GREAT MOMENTS IN SPORT :
Golf

GREAT MOMENTS IN SPORT:

Golf

MICHAEL McDONNELL

PAGURIAN PRESS LIMITED
TORONTO

© 1974 by Michael McDonnell
A Christopher Ondaatje publication. All rights reserved.
No part of this book may be reproduced in any form without
the permission of the publishers.

Printed and Bound in Great Britain

Library of Congress Catalog Card Number: 74–79600
ISBN 0–919364–61–6

PAGURIAN PRESS LIMITED
TORONTO

Distributed by:

PUBLISHERS MARKETING GROUP
A BAKER & TAYLOR COMPANY

Executive Offices
1515 Broadway
New York, N.Y. 10036

Distribution Center
Gladiola Avenue
Momence, Illinois 60954

FC-006

CONTENTS

CONTENTS

ILLUSTRATIONS

Chapter 1: *Arnold Palmer, Royal Birkdale, 1961*

As soon as he saw the crowd, Palmer knew it must be bad trouble. They clustered around the bush and peered solemnly like gawpers at some hideous accident. That, it most certainly was, for there had been no need for him to strike that drive so close to the corner of the sandhills. It had been an unnecessary attempt to set himself a more comfortable approach shot into the green. Against the wind, there was always a risk of drifting slightly, but disastrously, off course. Now it had happened.

It was too late for recriminations. What might have been was irrelevant. This was the only point from which to win, and he was much too close to let it all slip from him.

Rees, he knew, was inspired. He knew that feeling because it had happened to himself often enough. He knew also that when that kind of spirit possessed a man, he lost touch with reality and his powers and deeds verged on the miraculous, as plaguing doubts and fears diminished under a more powerful guiding force.

Rees, in this mood, could close the gap and go past before he realised the enormity of his act. He could be British Open champion before he realised how difficult that task should be. The Welshman's suicidal start that morning probably had been the reason for his subsequent blistering aggression. It had begun with a seven, and the frustration and anger of the setback compelled him to take his revenge on the course with a fearless retaliation, and this had endured, and then expanded into inspired golf.

Yet Rees's seven at least gave a Palmer a little space in

which to work. It was, in fact, the only thing that separated them, and Palmer was thankful for it. Yet he could not afford another error before he reached the clubhouse if he was to hold off the Welshman.

Of course, Rees did not have a monopoly of disasters. Palmer could look back on his own seven and ponder on the ironic justice of it all. Nobody else actually saw the ball move in that bunker. But he *knew* – and that was all that mattered. It had been a double-blow since not only did it distract him enough to thin the ball through the green, but also he was then obliged to accept a penalty stroke.

He had been commended afterwards for his honesty and it puzzled him that others should think there was any alternative action. If golf skill was the means of self-assertion over others, then the personal gratification from triumph – the entire point of it all – was lost if something other than skill was employed.

The joy of golf for him had always been that he could demonstrate his superiority with abundant clarity. It showed in the desire to thrash the ball farther than anybody else. That was his way. The whole thing had to be so apparent, there could be no doubt in his mind, nor in that of anybody else. That way, it was simple and tidy – but then that was his way in all things. The house at Latrobe, built piece by piece as he won the money, because he distrusted mortgages; his confusion and concern over the 'paper' wealth that his shrewd manager Mark McCormack had built for him because none of it offered as much comfort as cash in the bank.

Hitting a golf ball was simple enough; or rather, as a means of proving oneself, it was uncomplicated and depended on nothing outside one's own skill. Success was perfect since honour could not be shared, nobody else was involved. All men started equal, the slate clean, it was just a matter of proving that he was better than the rest.

That was, for him, the attraction of golf – and the reason why nothing else in life suited him better. His early days as a paint salesman had demanded concessions in attitudes that he could never make. That kind of success – the selling of gallons of paint – held no identifiable merit. It depended too much on others and their opinion of the salesman. Palmer needed to control his own fate and because of this, he made an awful salesman.

He came to professional golf when he realised there was nothing else. His background, from the days when he worked in his father's pro shop and there acted out fantasies that he was putting for the British Open, was designed to direct him towards the playing of golf.

Even if Deke Palmer, his father, had no serious ambition for his son, at least he instilled his own golf philosophy into the boy. Firstly, the ball had to be hit damned hard, and when that force was instinctive, it could then be harnessed and directed towards the target.

What emerged was not always a pretty sight because Palmer's crushing power demanded, by the laws of physics, that there was an equal and opposing force, and in his quest for power his left hand had to fight his right to avoid a monumental hook. Thus, the Palmer flourish – that finish to his swing with both hands fighting and the club waving like a lion tamer's whip – was copied disastrously by thousands who thought therein lay the secret of power.

Of course, the heavy rolling countryside around Pittsburgh where he had learned his golf made it imperative to hit the ball a long way. Perhaps, too, on this kind of forbidding terrain he first came to regard the golf course as an opponent – a foe that had to be overwhelmed rather than tricked into surrender. That was his style – to impose himself and his will on a golf course in the manner he intended.

He never questioned why this worked for him. Others could see the difference between Palmer and the rest, but could never identify the reason. There were plenty of players of equal skill and power, yet none could assault a golf course with the monumental effrontery that Palmer summoned. He could never explain it, other than as a matter of seeing what he had to do then doing it. Anyway, it was for others to find the equation. To him, there was no problem.

His legend took shape at Augusta in 1960, when Ken Venturi was already in the Press centre being interviewed as the new Masters champion, because nobody out on the course, it was thought, could catch him. But even as Venturi spoke, he was losing the title. Palmer wrought havoc on the last two holes and Venturi was left talking to himself as they went out to find the new champion – Arnold Palmer, by a stroke.

The legend gained strength that same year with the U.S. Open at Cherry Hills, when Mike Souchack was coasting to a comfortable triumph. Then, Palmer had ripped the course and Souchack's ambitions to shreds with a momentous last round. Why? It could not have been planned. Nobody could plan to remain dormant for three rounds of a championship, and then erupt savagely enough to win on the last day.

Palmer, it seemed, refused to accept fate, but instead imposed himself upon it. Others talked about the possibility of winning once they found themselves in a good position. Palmer, when the spirit moved him, made his own chances even if destiny had already pencilled in somebody else's name. It seemed that his will power and strength of purpose were as ferocious as his physical force.

Nobody could stand in his way, and at times he was prepared, if provoked, to take on the gods themselves if their plans did not coincide with his own. If this was arrogance then it was confined to a golf course. That was the only sector of his life in which he felt obliged to prove himself. Even when it was suggested that he run for governorship of his native state in later years, the idea did not interest him in terms of self-fulfilment.

The gods, that day at Birkdale, were beginning to get in his way again. The ball, now trapped by that bush on the fifteenth hole, was but another example of their perverse nature. But this aroused not so much despondency within Palmer as an irritable impatience that they would not leave him alone. This feud was long-standing and began a year ago at St Andrews, the home of golf, when he arrived with the U.S. Masters and U.S. Open titles under his belt, and such was his mood, he felt he could equal Hogan's Grand Slam of all three titles in one summer. All that remained was the British Open.

But Palmer failed by one miserable stroke. Others saw it as a brilliant performance, an outstanding display of skill and adaptability by a man who had never seen a links course before, nor played the smaller British ball before his experiences in the Canada Cup at Portmarnock the previous week. To Palmer, however, it was abject failure. To him the necessary skills had been learned. He was fully equipped but still he had failed.

He vowed that he would return to win, and Birkdale was the sequel, the year of revenge. Whatever fate had in mind for Rees or anybody else, did not really matter, because Palmer had come back for that title. Yet there were times when his insolence seemed to have angered the gods into vicious retaliation.

A savage gale ripped huge marquees from the ground and ravaged anyone who ventured outside. Palmer, it seemed, would have none of their nonsense and ploughed through it all. On another day, they sent a deluge, but Palmer waited patiently playing cards until the storm had passed. Then he recommenced his task of winning the Open.

Next came the moving golf ball in the bunker which cost him a seven and, earlier on the last day – during the third round – he had withstood another assault on the sixteenth hole. His approach shot had been too powerful and there was neither enough fairway nor green to save it. Only a bush halted it behind the green, and before Palmer reached the spot he prepared himself for an unplayable lie.

At first, he thought he was right. There seemed no route

13

through that foliage to the flagstick. And yet, as he stared, he suddenly noticed a small gap in the branches, just large enough for a ball to pass through. But it needed absolute precision and if he missed the ball would fall into worse trouble, perhaps even remain in the branches, and he would have thrown this championship away through his own over-presumption of skill.

And yet he could not afford to give away strokes. Just one shot, even now, could mean the difference between winning and losing at the end of the day. The shot was possible and was worth the risk involved. In any case, if it did not come off there was the possibility at least of repairing the damage over the rest of the day.

He selected his sand wedge and laid the blade open so that the face looked like the top of a huge nail driven into the ground. Then he jabbed quickly at the ball and it jumped clear without touching a twig, rose majestically, then dropped like a hawk on its prey. It spun and halted inches from the hole. Nagle, his playing partner, joined in the cheers because he had felt convinced that Palmer was staring down the throat of disaster and that, at best, he could not escape with fewer than seven or eight strokes on that hole.

That episode alone should have been enough torment for one day, but now, as he approached the crowd surrounding the bush in the last round, he knew that his agony was not yet complete. He moved through the crowd to examine the mess. The ball was in deep grass under a small bush, and his first glance up the fairway towards the green told him that, against the wind, it was virtually impossible to get home with one blow.

The frustration turned to anger. A wedge would be strong enough to chop the ball through the bush and move it forward, but that would mean a third stroke to reach the green, and would give Rees not simply the advantage of narrowing the difference, but the added incentive of knowing that Palmer was having problems.

Perhaps he could take a seven-iron – which, after all, he could wield like a wedge – to gain a few more yards and the chance of hitting his third stroke close enough for a single putt. He took the seven-iron, settled over the bush and was about to strike when the spell was suddenly broken. He stepped back and went across to the golf bag. The seven-iron was replaced and the spectators edged forwards to see what he was doing.

They assumed that he had accepted the difficulties of the stroke and had a reverted to a safer, shorter iron. But then they saw it . . . a six-iron. Palmer was attempting to get home and there was not another man in the world who would have dared such impudence. They were horrified – it was like watching a man select the weapon with which he is about to commit hari-kari. Everybody knew what would happen next . . . what could only happen next.

Palmer returned to the bush and his enormous hands, the fingers like bunched bananas, wrapped around the club. The stare was frozen into concentration and the mouth turned down at the edge as he prepared himself for the most audacious stroke of his life.

This was the essential Palmer – a hopeless situation in which only the near-impossible would suffice. The stroke itself was awesome enough but its implications were crippling. Palmer had to defy the laws of good sense, probability and physics, and endure the pressure and strain upon him to produce an unrepeatable stroke – because no other would do.

Even as he stood there, knees flexed, feet splayed, there was a compelling sense of power about the man; an inexplicable sense of force, even though he was motionless. His manner and presence gave clear warning of the savage swipe that would descend upon that ball within a few seconds.

Then suddenly, he was in action. There is no hint when Palmer begins to swing. Nagle waggles, Nicklaus begins to turn his head away from the ball, Player rocks into action. But not Palmer. Suddenly he is at maximum speed. The club flashed away and the shoulder came round viciously hard and obscured his chin. And then he was powering back at the ball with irresistible force. Nothing could stop this.

The steel blurred into the bushes and there were noises. The swish of scythed grass, snapping twigs, the crack, a solid crack. Even as the spectators heard it, the pleasing shudder in Palmer's arms told him he had made contact. Then it was not the sound – but the sight. A bush, airborne. Grass scattering around him. And somewhere the ball. But where?

Suddenly the air cleared and there it was, a black speck far away in the sky on its course to the green. Its height told Palmer that it would reach its target. But some of the people did not see the ball, because they were still staring in wonder at the hole in the ground where once a bush had stood.

Not even a tornado could have wrenched it free so cleanly. Some would swear afterwards that the ground shook beneath them as Palmer's club cleaved that bush from his path. Or maybe it was just the gods groaning their surrender, because Palmer was free of them at last and could proceed to his first British Open title.

He had never unleashed that kind of force at a golf ball; nor perhaps would he ever be called upon to do so again. It was brute strength, that was all he intended, but in that extreme moment, the discipline of the body joined forces with that strength to drill the ball on to the green. It was a most important stroke in the development of British golf. It bore Palmer to his first British Open and set a pattern by which other world-class Americans, who wished to stand comparison, had to follow. After Palmer, they all came.

The interest and status of the British Open was revived, to make it a major championship again in world golf. This had its spin-off benefits in greater patronage for the British professional game and so gave more young men the chance to attain higher standards of play.

Against that background, Tony Jacklin took his first

faltering steps towards an eventual British Open. Thus, by the shot as much as any other, Palmer that day changed the pattern of British golf.

The bush was never replanted. But the spot is marked by a plaque so that pilgrims will never forget the incredible power of this man Palmer – nor the debt which British golf will forever owe him.

Chapter 2: *Jack Nicklaus, St. Andrews, 1970*

It was finished. Now he must stand there and watch somebody else win. Nicklaus had been so certain of himself but there was Sanders on that last green, one short putt from the British Open.

There is no escape from that agony of despair when a chance has gone for ever. And the worst is to come: when the man is alone in the night and the overwhelming sense of loss assails him. There is no comforting hope for the next time, because the pain of the present hurts too much.

Of late that pain had been too persistent for Nicklaus. People said that he could win whenever he wanted beause his ability was greater than all the others. This time he had wanted desperately to win, and this time he had worked well enough for it. But there was Sanders, who had forced himself through from a legion of unknown men who had scrambled a week ago just to get into this championship. There he was, on the last green at St Andrews with that putt for the British Open title. Nicklaus forced himself to watch, hoping that Sanders would miss, yet knowing that he would not.

Sanders was nervous and was taking far too long to dismiss the hole. Already he had made mistakes, none of them lethal, but all of them sure signs that the tension had already invaded his confidence. Even so, he simply had to hold out over this last stroke. There was probably that much resistance left in him. So Nicklaus waited with a sense of loss.

The drive had been good enough, but Sanders had then stepped out of character. For a lifetime he had made a fortune by manoeuvring the ball around golf courses, fitting each stroke to the terrain. It was not pretty but it was effective, and that strategy should have led him to a pitch-and-run stroke across the Valley of Sin, a treacherous hollow, in front of that last green on the Old Course.

Yet, as he reached for his wedge, it was obvious to all that Sanders did not trust himself to finesse the ball, but instead wanted the relief of a swing which would allow him to hit the ball unthinkingly. He was trusting to mechanics when he needed artistry. And that dilemma was to bring about his downfall.

The ball had been lofted high into the air across the Valley but, in his fear, he had struck too hard and the ball skidded past the hole to finish up the hill at the back of the green. Each stroke now was presenting him with a more damning situation.

He knew that the ball would gather pace as he struck it down towards the hole and that, if he was too firm with it, the ball would slide past – perhaps far enough to put him in the Valley of Sin that he had tried so desperately to escape. If he was too cautious then he faced equally hideous problems, since he would then have another downhill putt – and no-body gives themselves one downhill when they really need it.

There was more fear than purpose in the putt when he struck it and the ball faltered towards the hole. And long before it got there it was slowing down, as if it were afraid to venture too far at this most important moment.

Three feet from the hole it seemed to forget its lines, and froze. It was impossible even now to think positively, even though Sanders still had this putt for the title, because so much of the last few minutes had shrieked of panic and doubt. He might just hang on to win, but there was no doubt that he was slipping.

This should have been the greatest moment of his life, not least because he had been written off by everybody yet had played himself back to within a pace of a major world title. In that moment he should have emerged from a trough of despondency and failure that followed the disintegration of his peculiar knee-high golf swing.

It occurred to others that his presence at the British Open was an act of self-indulgence, since there was nothing to suggest that his luck would change particularly on the Scottish links which flank the old town. In any case there were no privileges. Sanders had to join hundreds of hopeful golfers for the chance of a place in the championship. It was a cruel but unavoidable humiliation for a world-class player, yet he endured it with good grace.

Sanders, with astute perception, saw redemption in the British Open, since he knew that his skill lay in working the ball around a golf course, and that this talent, on a seaside links, weighed just as heavily as any stroke-making brilliance that others might bring to the championship. Thus he had more chance of regaining his prestige here than on an American course with its dart-board docility.

St Andrews, with its rugged and rather featureless terrain, was receptive to diligent workmanship. Sanders knew that he could get away with some indiscretions on that kind of course and that, if he could find the greens without too many incidents, he stood a fair chance, since his putting skill had not diminished. With only three feet of the championship left to be played, he was correct.

Yet Nicklaus was not the only man to watch this drama unfold on the last green with a sense of loss. Jacklin, fresh from his audacious triumph in the U.S. Open, came to St Andrews brimming with confidence, despite the draining rigours of a round-Britain T.V. match with Arnold Palmer.

In the first round Jacklin had moved upon the Old Course with lethal accuracy, and when he dismissed the first nine holes in 29 witheringly magnificent strokes, there were those among the townsfolk who feared that the legend of St Andrews would be left in tatters. Nothing on earth, it seemed, could prevent him from tearing the Old Course's reputation to shreds.

Nothing on earth did stop him. It was rain from heaven which poured in gallons and submerged this unforgettable exhibition of golf before the round had been completed; rain, that is, and a bush beside the fourteenth green into which his four-wood had drilled the ball. In the time he waited for a ruling on how to play the ball, the rains came furiously and play was suspended. The ball 'stayed' in the bush overnight, and Jacklin returned the next day to play it. But by then the magic had vanished.

There are those who say that Jacklin's wayward shot into that bush was caused by a distant shout which distracted him at the top of his backswing. Perhaps it was. But it is a wise maxim, which every club golfer knows, not to stand around swinging the club you intend to play when you are delayed. Something invariably goes wrong.

Jacklin was delayed on that hole while the preceding players negotiated the green. He stood there swinging the club, then felt obliged to chat to Norman Von Nida, from the press group, when Von Nida moved forward to talk. Others might have put the club back in the bag, cut the conversation short and waited, hands in pockets. But then who is to question the actions of a man who has just played nine holes in 29 strokes?

And yet that staggering setback was to take some of the heart out of his golf and, although he finished well enough, he did not regain the stride that could have made him champion. After that, he was always playing for a place.

This was not true of Trevino. Or rather it was, but he was playing for first place. But he played it all the wrong way. He led going into the last day, then made the wrong tactical decision. He tried to protect his lead and was conserving while others attacked. The danger of caution is that it tends to lead to greater disasters without the attendant redemption the attacker receives with occasional birdies. It was a lesson he learned the hard way, and he vowed as he lost the lead that he would not make the same mistake again.

As Nicklaus wiltered, the stage was clear for Sanders, who could permit himself four strokes down that last hole to beat Nicklaus by a stroke. It was tight but it was enough.

Then, as Sanders stood over that putt for victory, the desire to become champion again reawakened fully in Nicklaus. But now it was too late. Since 1967 he had not won a major title and some argued that he was simply bored with success and that no matter how hard he tried to give tournaments a sense of significance, his own hunger for triumph had gone. He was a millionaire, he had won all the titles too often, and was more interested in fishing and hunting.

As the title was escaping from him, Nicklaus suddenly realised how much it mattered, and how pointless it all was without winning. It was not money, for Mark McCormack, his manager at that time, had made enough shrewd investments so that Nicklaus need never work again. But then money had never been a problem. His father had been comfortably off in Columbus, Ohio, and Nicklaus had all the benefits. In fact there was a suspicion that his lack of popularity with the public stemmed from this as much as from the fact that he found winning so easy and that he was pushing their beloved Arnold Palmer from the throne.

From the start, when he had won the U.S. Open in his first year as a professional, his career had been a constant reminder to others that he was so far removed from the game they played that it could be called by a different name. His presence could 'psyche' the rest of the field into a damaging frame of mind.

Bobby Jones, one of the greatest influences in golf and the man who achieved the Grand Slam of four major titles in one summer, said of Nicklaus: 'He plays a game with which I am not familiar.' In fact it came to a state that, whenever somebody else won a championship, the public – and even the winner himself – figured that Nicklaus must be off his game that week.

Such esteem, which started from his childhood, was bound to have ill-effects. At first he was a little unsure of himself, and in his first year as a professional he came to Southport for a guaranteed sum to play a tournament. He was painfully polite, and assiduously courteous to a point of holding doors open to let other people through.

By the time he returned as a champion of world class, the courtesy had disappeared. It would, however, be difficult to tell whether the barren period which followed this phenomenal success was the cause of the maturing and mellowing process within Nicklaus because, such is the fickle world of journalism, there was really not much point in talking to him while he was not winning.

By the end of that championship at St Andrews he was to demonstrate clearly the change. He was to kill once and for all his cold superman image. He was to show that despite his genius he was no different from any other human being who seeks justification through sport and that triumph, the repeated proof of superior skill, was the only sustenance by which a champion could exist.

Sanders missed the putt. As soon as the club touched the ball, he knew that he had missed and had committed himself to a lifetime of regret. Even before the ball reached the hole, he leaned forward as if to rake it back and try again. The British Open, in the act of winning, had been lost.

Nicklaus could scarcely believe it. He had been given another chance. Sanders had none because not only would he have to confront Nicklaus the next day in a play-off but also he would have to fight the memories of the greatest lapse of his life.

The crowd felt sorry for Sanders because he had missed, and because you get only one chance to snare a sleeping giant and you have little chance when you dare to meet him face-to-face. Until that moment Sanders had been swept along by the hysteria of the last round. Now he would have to start cold against the world's most accomplished golfer.

There was enough evidence to show that Sanders had been inspired to a level he did not know he could achieve in that last round. On the Road Hole, the seventeenth, he had been bunkered beside the green and only an impossible stroke could deliver him from this pit. The ball had to climb quickly, but with measured pace and spin to land on the few blades of grass that separated him from the hole.

That was the moment when the tie with Nicklaus seemed inevitable, but Sanders, after an eternity of study, dug into the sand and through the spray, the ball climbed out to fall close, but not all that close, for a single putt to maintain his lead.

Tragically, such determination was wasted by his own errors on the last hole which he will relive a thousand times and wonder whether it was the putt, the approach or his own superstition which robbed him that day. The thought about superstition came later but it crossed his mind quickly at the time.

He has an aversion to white tee pegs, the reason is obscure but effect real enough. In that heady moment as he stood on the last tee, Trevino, his playing partner, handed him a white tee peg that belonged to the late Tony Lema who had won at St Andrews in 1964. It was meant as a gesture of encouragement and indeed Sanders hit a perfect drive. Only then did he notice that he had gone against his superstition. After that, there was too much to think about but late that night, he wondered about the tee peg.

After twelve holes of that Sunday play-off, Nicklaus had imposed himself on their encounter and was four strokes clear. Already some of the gallery had drifted back to the club house, since the only other item of interest would be Nicklaus's speech of thanks, and they wanted to be in position for it. Sanders, head bowed, could make no dent in this man's armour and was fast running out of time in which to do so.

Suddenly the break came – Sanders holed for a birdie on

the fourteenth and Nicklaus missed. It was not in itself significant, but when Sanders did it again on the next green the lead was suddenly down to two strokes and the crowd turned on their heels to rejoin the fight.

Nicklaus was unsettled by this mild counter-attack and lost his composure enough to blast too strongly towards the sixteenth green and put the ball well beyond the target. Minutes later, he trooped from that green with only one stroke protecting him from Sanders. That was how it remained until they reached the eighteenth tee.

Both knew that the Open championship rested on this hole and yet Sanders, as he stood first on the tee, seemed ill-equipped with that stumpy swing to contain the irrepressible force that Nicklaus was bound to deliver to his ball. If only he could lift his back swing a little higher to give the ball a real thump. As it was, he was almost airborne as he made contact with the ball, in his effort to grab every possible inch of fairway.

It was a magnificent blow which propelled the ball almost into the Valley of Sin. Nicklaus watched it, but gave no sign that he was impressed. What Sanders had achieved with a driver, he could equal with a three-wood. And yet ... a driver would certainly get him home. He knew that he could reach that green 358 yards away.

Yet the perils of failure far outweighed the advantages of reaching the green. Sanders might still get his three. What could Nicklaus hope for from a big drive – a two? If he failed, by the merest fraction to make correct contact with that ball, his hopes would rocket over the railings and maybe as far as the town centre itself. Certainly the British Open would be finished for him.

The waiting thousands watched silently, on each side of the fairway. The window of every building overlooking the course was crowded with anxious faces and, in the distance, some students hung precariously from their dormitory windows while Nicklaus mulled over the problem.

The big man began to move and nobody was quite sure what he was doing. Instead of walking towards his golf bag, he was struggling physically with himself. And then it became clear. He was removing his sweater, and that was the signal that he was 'going' for that green.

Never before, in his all-conquering career, had he been pushed so hard that one stroke would decide the outcome. His ambition hung on the precise execution of this next stroke. He reached out for the driver, and his caddie Jimmy Dickinson, as if not wishing to be a party to it, left Nicklaus to remove the club from the bag.

Nicklaus took a few practice swings and then gazed down the fairway as if imagining the ball on perfect flight to that green. Then he stepped up to the ball, this rock of a man, and visibly gathered himself for the most decisive stroke of his career.

Now, he was not looking at the green, but just glancing forward to a spot on the ground a few feet ahead of him. If he could deliver the ball over that spot, it would be despatched correctly. He was now imprisoned by his own concentration as he attempted to incorporate the accuracy of a wedge into his driver and hit a target the best part of a quarter of a mile away.

He seemed to take an eternity preparing himself – in fact it was only seconds – and as his head turned between ball and his target spot on the ground, we wondered whether the stray thought of caution would squeeze into his mind and compel him to put the driver back into the bag. But then he began to crank his head slowly to the right, a sure sign that the Nicklaus swing has already started in his brain. Then the club and arms began to move, and it was too late to think again. In a second he was wound tight as a mainspring, and suddenly the power was unleashed.

The explosion of power was frightening, and the act itself left its witnesses in a state of shock. At first nobody thought about the ball. When their eyes did scan the sky the ball was

too quick for them, and only those in the direct line of fire
had a chance of finding it in the sky. Has any golf ball ever
been fired into the air for so long? When it came to earth it
was only half finished with this hole, and it raced on like a
frightened fox.

For a second, the people behind the green thought that
they were in danger as the ball raced scornfully past
Sanders's effort, and through the Valley of Sin. The ball had
too much power to be slowed by the green, and raced on,
ignoring the flagstick until thick grass behind the green
snared it close to the boundary fence. Nicklaus, by the very
excellence of his stroke, had produced yet another crisis for
himself.

Ten minutes passed by, as the Open championship teetered
between both men. Sanders this time pitched and ran his
ball through the Valley, and it finished four feet from the
hole – by painful coincidence in almost the same position as
on the previous day. Then Nicklaus was the man with the
problems, because he could easily ruin himself as he tried to
escape from that long grass. His backswing was menaced
by the fence and the grass would cushion the force of the
clubhead so that he would have to strike firmly to break
clear. But how firmly? If it was too hard, he could find himself at the front of the green . . . or perhaps even in the Valley
of Sin.

He studied hard, settled himself, and made numerous
passes at the ball. Then, quite abruptly, he chopped into the
long grass and the ball broke free. His first worry was over
since he was clear, and then the second worry diminished as
he saw the slow pace of the ball. But his relief gave way to
panic as he realised that the ball would not have the strength
to cover the distance to the hole, and that he would face a
hated downhill putt, a longer more horrible imitation of that
which Sanders had missed on the previous day.

It was still Nicklaus to play, because Sanders's ball was
closer to the hole. Though he did not know it, Sanders had

already played his last effective stroke of the championship with that pitch and run. But he stood there, knowing that Nicklaus controlled both fates and there was nothing he himself could do ... if the big man holed this one it was all over.

Any other time, and with perhaps anybody else, the odds might have been in favour of Sanders surviving. His opponent faced a long, frightening downhill putt, for which the penalty of missing was painfully apparent. It was the end of a hard day, and each factor might have conspired towards the failure of any other man except Jack Nicklaus. And yet that was the only hope left for Sanders. It began to rise, joyfully, as he realised that Nicklaus, touched by the tension of it all, had struck the ball too hard.

Nicklaus himself stretched out his arm in anguish as he saw the ball moving too rapidly, and saw the slope of the green begin to drag it away from the hole too early in its journey. It was too fast for the hole to snatch it and yet.... The ball caught the rim of the hole and flicked down out of sight. Nicklaus joyfully threw his putter in the air and Sanders ducked as it came back to earth, narrowly missing him.

In that uninhibited gesture of delight, Nicklaus demonto the thousands around him that he cared deeply about winning; that it all still mattered. It was that unashamed expression of joy – the first he had ever shown – that made the public warm to him in a manner he had never allowed before.

Sanders, now cloaked in his own personal misery, forced a smile, but nobody would have blamed him if he had shown the tears. Both men wanted this title badly. For both, it offered a different but equally important means of salvation. When would Sanders ever get the chance again? He was the kind of golfer who had to take advantage of fate when it came his way. Nicklaus and the Palmer of old could impose their own wills on championships. Sanders could never do that. He could simply try to take his chances if they came.

However, the formalities were not yet complete. Sanders still had to putt out for his scorecard even though it was something of a hollow gesture. He was standing virtually on the spot from where he had missed a day before. As he stood there, nobody would have blamed him if he tapped the ball casually towards the hole.

But Sanders took his time, and it was obvious that he was trying to prove something to himself and anybody else who cared to notice. The ball fell, but it was a day too late. He was a shattered man and his mask of flippancy vanished in that moment of agony. Then he saw his wife Scottie in tears, and he fought back his own emotions to smile at her and slip back into the casual manner. But between them, each knew the depth of the pain that was hidden by that smile.

That evening, late, I was leaving the clubhouse. It was almost empty with the commissionaire at his place behind the desk in the entrance hall, when Nicklaus and his wife Barbara entered. He offered his hand to the man behind the desk and said : 'I just wanted to come back and thank you for all your help this week.' Then he was gone. A different man. Not the one who arrived at St Andrews that week. Not the same. Never again.

Chapter 3: *Ben Hogan, Carnoustie, 1953*

He had come to Carnoustie to win. Of that, he had no doubt. That was the job, pure and simple, and fate, destiny, good fortune were discounted from his calculations. What faced him was a practical task requiring industry and planning. It was the attitude of craftsmen who build houses. With the right materials, plans and labour there is no mystery nor surprise about the result. And if it is to be the best, then these ingredients have to be superior.

Nobody but Hogan could think of a championship in these terms. But then nobody but Hogan had ever reached that degree of awareness of the game. At some point in his life he had withdrawn from the world so that he was left with himself, a club, a ball and a course to conquer.

Perhaps it was a terrible price to pay for that degree of skill, because Hogan forced something from himself that went beyond diligence, fervour and even obsession. It took him into a lonely world where only he and the golf course existed – he and the task that he had to accomplish. Nobody else lived in that world.

It was not arrogance nor gross presumption of his destiny, because Hogan's vision never stretched that far, never beyond exerting complete mastery over the stroke that confronted him. The only judgement that mattered was his own, and there was none harsher.

He could never share himself with others since he, Hogan, existed only with a club in his hands. He had nothing else to offer, and if others pitied his loneliness then it was a mistake, because within him there was a fullness of life which excited him so much that each day he could not wait for the hours of sleep to pass so that he might return to his beloved clubs and his foe, the golf course.

The compulsion in the beginning may have been a simple desire for affluence or at least a better quality of life than that he had known as a caddie in Fort Worth, Texas. But at some time the original motive had been lost in what became a pilgrimage towards perfection – which seemed, at times, to make both money and titles superfluous.

He strove for absolute mastery of his mind and his body. He was tormented by its logical possibility since degrees of excellence were but evidence of mechanical efficiency of the body. From that, it was impossible to escape the theoretical conclusion that the human frame could be drilled, each muscle harnessed, to a repetitive flawless discipline.

To this impossible purpose Hogan devoted his life, and he came closer to it than any other man. He reached an awareness and understanding of the golf swing that went beyond mechanics and, with his interminable drill on the practice ground, he acquired an exhaustive self-knowledge. He would tire himself deliberately to study his swing and attitudes in a state of fatigue. It was objective observation, as if he were studying some other specimen.

In the early days this obsession did him little good anu served only to frustrate him because at times it was possible to lose sight of the game's object and be distracted by the quality of strokes played. The successful man has few weaknesses, but those he possesses, he protects and ensures that they are never exposed. Hogan could not tolerate a weakness and would pick at it.

It took him ten dispiriting years before he was adequately equipped to become a champion, and by then he could drill the ball to whatever sector of the sky he wished to whatever blade of grass he selected. That was the art and the satisfaction. Its application would bring the rewards.

It seemed that most of his triumphs were simply the balance of this equation, in which rewards equalled work done. But that had changed at Oakland Hills because that U.S. Open title was always more than a question of superiority. There, the doubt was whether he was to be robbed by fate of the achievements that his lonely years of dedication had promised.

Just a year earlier, in 1949, he had been invincible and collected thirteen tournament wins, including the U.S. Open and the U.S. Masters titles. Then out of the fog on his way home from Pheonix, a bus crushed his body and forced all but the last breath of life from it.

But the body refused to die. The legs and pelvis were shattered and might never function again and, at best, the doctors suspected he would end his days in a wheel-chair, plagued by the thoughts of what should have been. It was not until then that the earlier frustrating years of Hogan, when he sought absolute mastery of his body, took on their real significance. Hogan had already decided that these shattered pieces would function again; that this body which now trapped him with its frailty would not only stand and walk again – but also that it would play golf as well as before.

That resolution had been made in his darkest moment, when he was capable only of a slight turn of his head. Had he wanted to scale Everest in that condition, the task could not have been greater. Yet he held a furious intolerance of his infirmities which was made even stronger by the memories of what he had achieved.

Not even his wife realised the extent of his will, nor did she know that when he was left alone in his room in later days he would force himself out of bed and drag himself, through blinding agony, in an effort to walk. Nor did she know that he had concealed a putter under his bed, and would practise the stroke when nobody was around.

This secret work with his putter was a sign to himself that the recovery was inevitable and that already he should begin working on what had been his only incurable weakness – his putting. Whatever Hogan had achieved had been despite his putting, and some remarked that his phenomenal accuracy with other clubs was but compensation for this inability to putt to even a reasonable standard.

In truth he considered putting a different game and one that held no interest for him. It must just as well have been baseball or football, so far removed was it from what he considered the fundamental art of golf. His disdain for the gifted putters of this world was clear enough, and he was once to remark to Bill Casper, a genius with that club: 'If you couldn't putt you'd be selling hot dogs outside the ropes.'

But, imprisoned in that room with his infirmities, Hogan was already intent that his putting should have the longest recuperation. During this period, hundreds of letters began to arrive, from people he had never known, wishing him a quick recovery and offering the clear message that they cared.

It was a new experience for Hogan, and one which nonplussed him. It was not that he disliked people, but rather that he was totally unaware of them outside his own small circle, and even there friends were accepted only on Hogan's terms. There was, for example, only one bedroom at Hogan's home because he did not like overnight guests.

People, or rather the public, were totally irrelevant to Hogan's view of his life and his work. At a golf course, they were eavesdroppers and, as far as he was concerned, unwelcome guests. His task was to conquer the golf course, and he disliked people looking over his shoulder so much that it would not have mattered to him if nobody turned up. In fact he would have preferred it that way.

He remained aloof from the crowds, and if he deigned to speak then the conversation would be monosyllabic, and he insisted, most times that he played, on being protected by a man carrying a banner which ordered 'No Cameras!' If they must watch, then it could be only on his terms. He had no need of the crowd.

But Hogan had misjudged them, and while his public accepted that he was a dour, grey, unapproachable man they saw also the overpowering dedication of a man towards his art. As much as the outstanding achievements this brought, it was this strength of will power for which they respected – and perhaps loved – Hogan.

Now he was discovering this truth, yet he was baffled by it. He had been locked too long within himself to change or soften, too tightly bound in his own character to mellow into a warmhearted idol. But now he was aware of this deep affection and could never again shut the public out of his life. It was as if then, when he was most helpless, that he realised his obligations to the public that his talent imposed. The truth was that any achievement needed a judgement other than one's own.

The close brush with death, the threat of infirmity, the time away from golf and now this unabashed national esteem, certainly brought a new dimension to Hogan's life. But it also served to drive him more desperately towards the only way he could justify himself – by playing golf.

At first he had moved to the quiet parts of his local golf course and ensured that nobody but the caddie could see his first pathetic efforts at a golf swing. He had to build afresh, because the bones had healed his frame to a new physique and there was the pain which would rarely leave him.

His first blows brought tears to the caddie's eyes, because this man remembered the real Hogan, not this bent cripple who was vainly trying to lift a sledge-hammer of a golf club. But if the caddie was not prepared for these pathetic efforts, then Hogan certainly was, and once again the ruthless demands he had always made of himself began to piece together a golf swing through the pain of a thousand strokes. He could feel life flooding back into him, as the silent affinity between himself and a golf ball began to exist again.

Within a year, his legs strapped for strength, he filed his entry for a tournament, and if the old Hogan might have thought the crowds had arrived to see a freak, he knew now that they were with him and not against him.

Though his stamina was weak and his competitive shell still fragile, he emerged after four rounds with the best score, but realised that Snead might equal it. He prayed that Snead would beat it, because he felt weak at the prospect of a play-off. As far as Hogan was concerned he had already passed the test and winning did not really matter that much now. But Snead forced him into a play-off and Hogan lost.

Before the U.S. Open at Oakland Hills, he felt restored enough to match anybody and even during that week, although he was assailed by crippling cramps which any number of hot baths and massages could not subdue, he remained among the leaders as they moved into the last round.

For a period in that last round his body was so racked with pain that he was on the verge of giving up. There was too much confusion, too many people with an equal chance, that he might force himself back into hospital without even the consolation of the title.

Yet, though his will was weakening, it still fought to retain the discipline of a lifetime over his body, and it prevailed long enough to force Hogan into a play-off the next day. Then he won, and this time he did not resent sharing his triumph with the thousands who came to watch.

Within three years, he came to Carnoustie, and the task was to win the British Open, because so many of his friends had urged him to extend the evidence of his talent by proving that he could win in alien conditions as other great men – Hagen, Jones, Sarazen – even Snead – had done.

It had never occurred to him before, because it was not an ambition that bothered him. But that year he already had the U.S. Masters and the U.S. Open, and once he had allowed himself to be persuaded about the British title, he pursued the task with scrupulous diligence.

He walked into a hotel in Carnoustie ten days before the championship was due to start, then, a minute later, walked out again because there was no bathroom attached to his bedroom. It proved to be a fortunate deficiency since it meant that Hogan was installed in a house in Dundee, away from the crowd. He could now devote himself fully to the process of preparation, and nobody would ever go into a championship better prepared than Hogan.

At first he simply gazed at the course as if assessing its character and strength. He studied every bunker and walked round them studying the texture and the shapes. He walked the course in reverse order – from greens to tees – to acquire a different perspective of each hole.

Then he went to work on his golf swing, working and working, to become accustomed to the new feel of the smaller British golf ball on his club blade, learning to accept the tightness of these seaside lies, and knowing within inches the precise range of each club, no matter what the conditions.

He would play countless shots to every green, learning the safe routes and avoiding the dangers. He would fire drives to various points on the fairway to discover the best angle of attack for each hole. Nothing was left to chance, since winning was a calculated process of producing the lowest score.

He was to be seen many times during those ten days, just standing on a tee, sometimes for a quarter of an hour, looking down the fairway as if trying to imprint the vision of the perfect strokes on his brain, like an actor learning his lines.

By the time that he was summoned to the first tee for the opening round he had a detailed vision of his route around Carnoustie, and he seemed to tread somewhere between the vision of that perfection and the reality of the day with all its marginal variations. He had learned his lines well and had drilled himself into a repetitive efficiency in which each stroke had been rehearsed a thousand times between his mind and the practice ground. It was as if the real act of judgement for each stroke had been taken long before he reached that first tee.

Yet this scale of preparation seemed preposterous, since it

was impossible for a man to handle all the perils of Carnoustie for three days on his own terms. Hogan had rehearsed every move to near-perfection but what would happen if that machine backfired? Had he the flexibility to cope with a crisis, and perhaps produce a stroke that had never been part of his campaign plan? Certainly he would have to fight hard, at some time, for his scores. He would be compelled to exert his powers of escape from the countless ambushes that this course had waiting for all of them, and it would be this ability to maintain his excellence when other forces were dragging him down that would weigh as heavily as that excellence itself.

On the first day, it was not perfection that he offered against Carnoustie, and the battle had been a long one. When it was almost over he faltered slightly, and was trapped twice by the bunkers he had studied so assiduously. It left others at the front of the field to live in hope of taking this title.

It did not bother Hogan, since he had now focused on his foe, the course, and if it were beaten thoroughly enough it was logical to assume that the title would follow. In any case it was the achieving, the process itself more than the result, which drew him. Afterwards there was only satisfaction and pride, none of which could equal the thrill of the act itself, the fashioning of the strokes to conquer each hole.

Thus, by lunch-time on the third day, with one round left to play, Hogan considered himself to be alone, even though Rees, Thomson, De Vicenzo and Cerda were pressing close. The mathematics did not tell the true story because that lunch-time De Vicenzo already knew that he had lost, and sobbed quietly in his hotel room. Some fatalistic insight told him that, with his pathetic putting, he could not possibly withstand the pressures to come.

Hogan moved upon that course in the afternoon as though he already knew he had an appointment with the trophy, and was in complete command of himself and Carnoustie. Each round had been progressively lower, more incisive, as if it had always been his plan to inflict slow torture on the reputation of the great golf course.

If that was the case, then the victim made one final defiant thrust in its death throes, when his approach shot towards the fifth green began to drift slightly from its planned route and the 15,000 people who had gathered to see Hogan win gasped in horror as they saw the fate of the ball.

The penalty was grossly out of proportion to the error, because he was no more than 25 yards from the green yet his ball hung on an upslope, half in sand and half in grass. That next stroke would require a blend of so many skills – the adjustment for an uphill stroke, the precision of a bunker stroke but the correct strength to hit through grass ... he had to judge the distance to the pin and assess the amount of halting spin he could impart on the ball. Each demand was formidable in itself, but now Carnoustie had conspired to present all of them to Hogan in a single stroke.

The cigarette smouldered, he squinted intensely at his problem and walked between the ball and the green count-less times, looking at both. His eyes and his brain had already seen the stroke needed and this information was now being passed to every muscle in his body. It took him four minutes before he was ready.

He took his nine-iron knowing that his brain and hands had to be aware of every fraction of space the clubhead covered on its path to the ball; that the grass must be grazed only slightly with the descending blow; that the force of it all must be precisely judged. He settled, and glowered a few more times at the flagstick.

The act itself, for it was not really a swing, began gently, then he was moving down towards the ball. Such was the gentleness of the caress between club and ball that the union seemed protracted like a lingering kiss. But then the ball rose, touched the green and stayed low. Then it moved onwards and disappeared down the hole.

It should have been, if not disaster, then at least a setback which demanded some penalty. But it was neither, since Hogan had turned that crisis into a simultaneous declaration of skill and dedication to the annihilation of a golf course. He emerged at the end of the round with a course record which was perhaps the real satisfaction that day at Carnoustie for Hogan. He won the British Open. He had done what they asked. He would not come back, because what else was there to prove?

Chapter 4: *Tony Jacklin,*
Royal Lytham and St. Annes, 1969

The trance began the night before and lasted all through the next day. It had been self-induced, but even when the effect of the sleeping pills wore off, Jacklin was drugged, protected from reality, by the very fantasy of the moment itself. He had switched off that part of his brain most vulnerable to the daggers of panic and doubt; or rather, it had switched itself off. And though he did not know it at the time, this is the priceless gift which separates the truly rare men from the ordinary.

This is how they must all react to the crushing strain of a task which seems too big to handle and against which they feel inadequate. By what other means is it possible to prevail when every force, even one's own resolve, has to be fought and contained every inch of the way?

But was it possible to take that gigantic step which would separate him for ever from the good, but ordinary, men who surrounded him and from whom he had sprung? Nothing would ever be the same again if he could force himself through the long alley of turmoil that the rest of the watching world saw only as the last round of the 1969 British Open championship at Royal Lytham and St Annes.

There was too much on which to ponder, too many sleepless possibilities. So he had returned to his rented house that night with a two-stroke lead and swallowed a couple of sleeping pills. Tomorrow was inevitable and too awful to contemplate. It, and his task, were unavoidable. Better that the hours, unconsciously endured, delivered him to it without the agony and torment of a hundred imagined disasters.

Of course, it had all been a little surprising because the last three days had offered no definite hint of waiting glory, but had resembled thankless hammer-and-chisel work on a reluctant piece of stone. He had not been playing well, and there was neither sweetness nor ease of purpose in his swing. The weeks before, in America, had been pathetic, and the rewards small. There had been nothing to suggest that the journey home would change that gloomy mediocre pattern. And so he came to Lytham, accepting inwardly that it was at best a charade, a token appearance which would be acted out in determined fashion for the benefit of those who believed he was Britain's best, perhaps only, hope.

What he did not realise was that this workmanlike mood, this inward acceptance that it would be hard work all the way, was the perfect base upon which to build a victory. He was not immediately ambitious, and thus he was not disappointed when the run of play went against him and he found himself labouring through sand traps almost as often as fairway. After all, what else could he expect, the way he had been playing?

Successful golf at Lytham is essentially a war of attrition. It is impossible to avoid trouble on the narrow links, particularly with the fire power the modern professional golfer brings to the game. Lytham is pock-marked with bunkers, swathed in scrub and buffeted by wind and frequent rain. Because of this, it affords a searching test of a man's resolution and character, since he must live with the prospect of disaster on every hole and endure and escape the occasional brush with it if he is to triumph.

Thus, the curious paradox of Lytham was that it proved most daunting to the man who arrived with what he considered an obedient swing and accurate marksmanship. Since trouble was inescapable, it damaged more the men who were not prepared, that week at least, to struggle for their golf. It is a simplification which does not fit every case, yet the ability to cope with setbacks weighed more heavily in this championship than any artistry.

A man, ill at ease with his golf swing yet compelled to make his living, always finds a way. More than this, he learns a nodding acquaintance with the trouble, which thus loses some of its terror. While this does not suggest that the best golfers in the world are not competent to deal with bunkers, a sense of injustice that a good stroke has been punished can make all the difference between a good and a bad recovery: the difference between willing the ball into the hole, because that is the only means available, and missing.

Whatever merits posterity attaches to an achievement, the winning of tournaments and even championships is a finely balanced, fragile thing, which depends as much on the mundane things – as trivial as burnt toast, a cold in the nose or a tiff with the wife. In other words, it depends on even the slightest change in a man's mental approach. Jacklin's mood was such that he expected no favours from fortune that week.

There is a hole at Lytham – and it doesn't matter which one – where Jacklin demonstrated his complete repertoire of qualities and deficiences. The drive had been hooked behind a sandbank, which was no great disaster since he could punch the ball clear from the soft sand and scrub with a short iron and find the fairway from which he could attack the green for a possible birdie or, at worst, a par five. Jacklin bustled round the ball, tight-lipped, walked to the brow of the hill and stared at the green. Then he came back and reached out to remove the head-cover from his wood. His caddie Willie Hilton glanced at him quickly but said nothing. It was definitely not the club to play, since, from the untidy lie, a wooden club demanded perfect contact, which in itself implied a mastery which, all week – and by that very drive – Jacklin had shown he did not possess.

If he was a fraction of an inch too low, the club would

bore into the sand (always assuming he could force the club-head through the stubborn grass which surrounded the ball). And good contact meant that the ball had to be taken cleanly and therefore it would come out low – too low to clear the sandbank a few yards ahead of him.

Jacklin settled himself over the ball and suddenly his swing lurched into life. He laid into the ball hard and it fizzed solidly into the sandbank, popped painfully into the air, and, with its last breath, disappeared just over the other side.

Club in hand, he charged after it and, as he reached the brow, saw that the ball was now trapped beside a young sapling. This was a disaster of his own making. There was a brief dialogue about whether he could lift without penalty from the tree, but before it was resolved he decided that he had stared at the ball long enough, and that to look longer would only increase the difficulties.

He took an iron and aimed for the fairway. Not only was it impossible to reach the green, but Jacklin could not even direct the ball towards it since his swing was dictated by the sapling. He lashed hard, the ball rose free, then dwelt on the fairway some distance from the green.

That third stroke could have nestled close to the flagstick or at worst been on the green, but he had been too greedy and had demanded too much from that treacherous lie. His desire to attack was commendable, but his discretion had been suspect.

He wedged, without apparent purpose, to the green and the distance the ball finished from the hole seemed to under-line that carelessness. He settled quickly over the putt and jabbed at the ball which scuttled across the green like a frightened mouse and disappeared into the hole. There was no sign of excessive emotion from Jacklin. Rather, he appeared to expect it.

It was a par five and there had been no damage to his score-card; no reason to think about that hole again since it had neither helped nor hindered his cause. Yet it had demonstrated the dogged nature that was to take Jacklin to the championship.

It was ever thus that week, and there were countless escape stories. Indeed in the third round, when he forced himself to the front of this international field, it seemed, over the last four holes, that it was impossible for him to recognise a fairway. He delivered his golf ball just about everywhere but along the route the architect intended.

The fifteenth at Lytham is about as accommodating as the top of a brick wall with marginally more room. He drilled his tee shot down there and the ball finished on the upslope of a hillock. Again, he reached for his wood, and even the hackers shuddered at their own memories of the disasters which follow attempting too much from an uphill lie.

Sure enough, the ball took off high and, as it lost its momentum, the hooking spin took command and forced it down into the crowds behind the railings. He pitched his next stroke towards the green, but it was a pathetic gesture and the ball flopped weakly into a bunker.

Jacklin trudged after it, no emotion showing save a tight-lipped alertness. He stepped into the bunker, glowered at the flag, then swung lazily through the sand to deposit the ball less than 12 inches from the hole.

Then he baffled Willie, his caddie, again as they stood on the next tee. All week, he had trusted his one-iron to thread the ball with adequate power through this narrow strip between the foothills. This time he reached for his driver, and for a moment Willie thought he had made a mistake and forgotten just where he was.

But Jacklin ripped into the ball with his driver almost as a contemptuous gesture to the memory of the troubles this course had caused him. He was like a Gulliver breaking free, and the ball was so far removed down that fairway that the birdie was inevitable.

This freedom was short-lived, for the next moment he was charting an apparently suicidal route through the rough of the following hole. A hooked drive delivered him there and an eight-iron served no purpose other than to gain a few more yards of rough towards the green.

In the manner of a dishevelled, beaten hacker he trooped after the ball, club still in hand, as if he really could not bother to assess which club might be correct for the next stroke and this one was as good as any. He used it and the ball skidded defiantly through the green and into a bunker. He coaxed the ball clear and left it dead against the flagstick for a five that had always seemed impossible.

There was another bunker awaiting him on the last hole as he struck his approach to the green, but again he came out and holed a demanding middle-distance putt for his par-four. Only then did he realise that all the others, and in particular O'Connor and Charles his nearest challengers, had found problems in greater measure and were behind him. Jacklin was on his own.

He said : 'I couldn't think too much. I just played every shot as it came. Mostly they came in bunkers and behind bushes. I don't want any more of that drama.'

It was a prayer rather than a statement, because Jacklin just wondered whether a stubborn refusal to submit to disaster could be enough to win the British Open the next day. That had been his pattern for three days. How could he expect a change now? Was it possible to win in retreat ... on the premise that everybody else might be retreating just a little quicker? It did not bear thinking about. It was a night for sleeping pills.

But why Jacklin? Why, of all the golfers that Britain had produced, some more naturally gifted, had this young man forced himself to the threshold of a breakthrough that none of them, save Faulkner 18 years earlier, had managed?

His most important quality was his capacity for growth, mainly in his attitude towards himself. Too many British golfers of equal ability had been stunted by their own in-flexible attitudes, so that it became impossible even to consider themselves capable of rising above the pack. This may have been due, in part, to the British way of life, which considers that the individual is of lesser importance than the mass; a philosophy which manifests itself in so many team games and the doctrines of team spirit and conformity which bedevil so many lives.

In a sense, Jacklin's predecessors lacked the ability to take their talent seriously, to regard their potential as limitless (as for some it most certainly was). Their self-evaluation was inflexible, as though they were satisfied with what they possessed and would venture no farther; rather like a swimmer who remains in the middle of the pool for fear of getting out of his depth. The obstacle was never really skill for these men, but a suffocating sense of inadequacy.

It was not that Jacklin, by some mystical insight, spotted this flaw and decided to avoid it. He was but a product of his generation in which individuality – and youth – had become important factors. It was a generation which saw no reason not to grab at instant success or its rewards. Patience was no longer a virtue but a stifling inhibition. There did not have to be a long apprenticeship of frustration before success could be well-earned.

This was partly climate and cause for the development of Jacklin. In the early days his ego had outweighed his skill and while attendant failures delighted his critics, the balance was correct. Skill can be acquired but a champion's ego, the motivating force, is with the man long before the two are matched. That kind of monumental self-confidence can never be acquired – not in the measure that a champion requires.

Of course, in its early form, it can be 'identified' as arrogance or the simple need to show off. And it may remain either or both these things without a proportionate development of skill. It was quite understandable for Jacklin's colleagues to laugh at his flashiness when he broke away from the baggy grey-flannelled tradition to wear gold-flecked

46

trousers; or to curse him to hell, as I have done, when he roared past in his bright red Cortina with his thumb pressed hard down on the hooter.

All of these were glimpses of an ego which was to transform his life and improve playing standards and boost the livelihoods of every professional – and anybody else connected with golf – in Britain and the rest of Europe.

Part of his development had to embrace the United States – not simply because he could learn his craft there, but because his ego demanded it. It followed, therefore, that he could embrace that style of life in a wholehearted manner and more unreservedly than any other of his fellow professionals. In his first years there, he thrilled to be part of the chromium-plated world which he had glimpsed previously only on film and television screens.

Add to this, his chameleon-like quality of adapting to his surroundings and it becomes clear that he was the perfect pupil to learn about, and benefit from, the American arena of golf. He was a gifted mimic, or rather had the facility to learn quickly by watching others. In a very short time, Jacklin was able to cope with the Americans, their golf technique, their playing attitudes and, so complete was his conversion, even their accent and manner of speech.

In terms of his British Open ambitions, he had achieved another important quality by his American commitment. He acquired a perspective on the championship which, in the mind at least, diminished it to a manageable proportion. Henry Cotton had found a similar answer after striving unsuccessfully to win the title. Only when he had spent time out of the country did he achieve a freshness and new attitude towards the title and, in so doing, win it.

There has always been the suspicion that many British players could have won their own championship if they had not thought it quite so important; if it had not loomed quite so large that it dwarfed their aspirations so that, at best, they could only hope rather than intend to win it.

47

This theory stood a further test, since the Americans, with all their experience of equally lavish tournaments, could regard the British Open as just another event and therefore not be frightened by it. The same attitude could not apply among British players, since for them there was nothing to equal the pomp and circumstance of a British Open.

When Jacklin returned he was, to all intents and purposes, a visiting 'American'. He had won a tournament there and was making a handsome living, certainly better than he could expect from the British circuit. Thus he, too, had some measure of this detachment when he came to the British Open and if not quite to the same degree as the true American, then at least it was enough to let him breath a little easier.

He slept nine hours before they woke him and told him it was time to start the most important day of his life. He had already accepted that there was no point in calculating the possibilities; that he would drive himself mad with permutations of fate and that it was useless to attempt a plan for his last round. He had to play and trust to fortune. Winning was as much what other people did as what he could produce, and he had no power over them.

True enough, that day they were all to think, for a moment at least, that they could win. De Vicenzo, the balding patriarch, made a sprint for the lead but was foiled on the return run. O'Connor began to waste putts and saw his chances vanish while Thomson and Nicklaus watched countless birdie putts graze the hole and ruin their hopes. But these were personal and private miseries about which Jacklin would never know.

Charles, his playing partner, was also his nearest challenger and, if nothing else, could be used as a pacemaker. But Charles began to submit on the first hole when he missed the green with his tee shot and allowed Jacklin to move father away.

Although Jacklin was to miss fairways and find trouble

as he had done on the other three rounds, he concentrated even harder on maintaining the rhythm of his swing, because he knew that this would keep at least a few of his strokes straight and cut down some of the waywardness that the tensions of the moment were producing.

It has always been his weakness, in a crisis or when playing extremely well, to hit hard with an eagerness that sends his golf swing into action at a ferocious and damning pace. That day he forced himself to swing at an even tempo, and as they turned at the far end of the course, by the railway station, for the run back to the clubhouse, he sensed that he had only himself to beat. Charles was on hand to pick up the pieces . . . but there would not be any pieces if Jacklin kept his game together.

Charles had his last significant chance on the long fifteenth hole, when Jacklin, now resolved to hold his three-stroke lead with an ill-fitting caution, reached for his putter to knock the ball 50 feet towards the hole. It was much to ask of a putter and Jacklin left the ball so short of the hole that he missed the next one. But Charles was not ready to accept the gift, and missed his own putt that would have brought them closer. Jacklin missed another putt on the next green, but by then even Charles knew that it was too late.

Thus Jacklin stood on the last tee of the British Open with a two-stroke lead. His first instinct was to steer the ball safely, and the thought flitted across his mind that three wedge-shots would see him on that green. But the idea was gone almost before he had considered it. A similar thought had occurred to him when he held the lead on the last tee at Jacksonville, the scene of his first triumph in America.

It was an outrageous thought anyway. This was the British Open with millions watching. He had to win like a champion at least here on the last hole. He reached for his driver and Willie Hilton's stomach turned at the memories of the disasters that this stick had brought them all week. More than ever, Jacklin's tempo mattered now.

The crowd hushed as he locked himself into a cocoon of concentration then swung back easily, almost paused at the top, then let fly, arms and club chasing the ball into a high sweeping flourish. Within seconds, the crowd began to cheer. The ball had been launched on a perfect course towards the fairway.

Now there was only one stroke remaining that could possibly go wrong before he could be champion. He selected his seven-iron and without fuss, moved lazily, but firmly, on the ball. It took off, and his first anxious glance told him all he needed to know. His eye took in the mounds on either side of the green, and he knew his ball was between them – dead centre.

Not until he reached the green did he know how close he was, because the crowd broke through from the railings as he played the stroke and swarmed around him. But their cheers told him now how good it was, and he took the time to wave to them as he marched towards the green between the grandstands.

Two putts later, he was British Open champion. He threw the ball into the crowd. It was to be the start of a financial fortune that would lead to a Rolls-Royce and a stately home. He had changed the pattern of British golf and lifted it from the doldrums. He had stepped into the champion's class and had done it in a most courageous manner. It had not been a demonstration of flawless and superior stroke-making. But nobody had shown more determination, tenacity and stubborness in the face of so many opposing forces.

Nobody fought harder that week. In a way Jacklin was the kind of champion his own people preferred – a man with guts to believe in himself and fight against the odds. In the Press tent afterwards, our typewriters clacked furiously as we pounded out the news. The man at the next typewriter was Peter Thomson, writing his daily piece. Only a few minutes earlier, he had been in the thick of the battle. He turned to me and said: 'Nobody knows how close I came. It was not a close-run fight. Tony is good but not yet great. We shall have to wait for that.'

The pattern of the conflict was none of Jacklin's making. All that mattered was that he had succeeded where others of greater pedigree and experience had failed. Milton had some words for it :

> 'All is not lost; th' unconquerable will,
> And courage never to submit or yield :
> And what is else not to be overcome?'

Chapter 5: *Lee Trevino, Royal Birkdale, 1971*

What an awful mess. And what a stupid, stupid way for the most inspired month of his life to end. Here on a sandhill overlooking the Irish Sea. Thousands of miles from Merion to Montreal to here and this goddam sandhill. And just over the hill, the prize was waiting for him. Not just the British Open but the glory of winning all three – the U.S. Open and the Canadian Open as well – inside four weeks.

He was clear of them all, and what remained of Birkdale should have been an undemanding ritual with Lu, the Formosan, in attendance as runner-up. It had all seemed easy. Surely history should be tougher than this.

He set himself to the ball, as he had done a million times, on that seventeenth tee, and felt the comforting tight turn of his shoulder and the thrust from his legs into the ball. It was an easy swing because he knew that the ball would clear the towering sand peaks to find the fairway on the other side.

He watched the ball begin its familiar route through the air. It was low and left, then it climbed and soon it would drift back towards the middle of the fairway. And then it would drop like a stone. His stomach twisted in growing panic as he realised the ball was not coming back.

This time it had forgotten the routine and seemed determined to head on, in suicidal treachery, towards the hills as if prepared to sacrifice itself to ruin Trevino when he was so close to the prize. Then it was gone beneath the willow scrub and the grass. He waited for a sign of life, a movement that could mean his ball had tumbled down the bank. But there was none. A mountain climber would find it hard to keep his foothold up there. What chance could Trevino now have of making a stroke? So much distance was still needed.

He knew before he reached the peak that there would be no chance of a full swing, no possibility of using the club he needed. Maybe no chance of a swing at all . . . no chance of finding it. But he walked briskly, outwardly calm, towards the disaster, because he knew that Lu was watching him.

Both knew it was a suicidal stroke, and Lu was the only other man in this championship to whom this disaster had any importance, because the Formosan was the only man remaining with the remotest chance of catching Trevino over what little remained of this Open.

The irony of it escaped Trevino because his mind was full of other things. But in the past few weeks he had beaten the best players in the world and even taken the U.S. Open from Nicklaus in a play-off. Now here he was on the threshold of another triumph but about to make it so difficult for himself that Lu, who did not approach the class of the men Trevino had beaten, was already suspecting he might pick up the pieces. If that happened, Trevino himself would have dealt himself the blow that ruined the star and dragged the surprised and unready understudy from the wings.

At best this was to be another messy kill. He was like a bullfighter who bungled it and made the bull take a long time to die. Neither the Canadian nor the U.S. Open had been won inside the distance. Maybe it would happen again here.

It had started at Merion with a putt on the last green that would have given outright victory, but a noise from a spectator had unsettled him and he missed. The next day he faced Nicklaus in a play-off over 18 holes, and even though he respected this man as the best in the world, somehow the ordeal was manageable.

Long before Trevino became a tournament professional, he had lived by his wits and skill against anybody who would play him for money. His business ranged from the municipal course in Dallas to the local pitch-and-putt, where his speciality was to take on all-comers for cash, using himself only a taped-up bottle with which to hit the ball. On a good week, he could take home 100 dollars.

That kind of living developed a vicious skill and with it the supreme faith to be sure what he could do with a golf ball, particularly in those gut-tearing moments when a putt had to be sunk and all could be lost on the turn of the ball. But more than this, he learned about human nature and how it reacted to whatever pressures applied. Thus while he respected Nicklaus, he could regard him simply as an opponent. Their encounter would be match play and while it is not possible to exert absolute control on an opponent, it is feasible that one's own play brings pressure to bear.

These two men had a professional respect for each other. They were from different worlds, yet were united by their talents on a golf course. Nicklaus had been the crown prince and was now king. Trevino had read about Nicklaus's exploits long before Nicklaus knew that Trevino existed. Nicklaus had been groomed in the air-conditioned world of the country club to a status in world golf where even the establishment sought his advice. Trevino had been a shrill gate-crasher into this cool, sophisticated world.

So long as his talent remained, he would be tolerated by the blue blazer brigade as a character – which meant that he had to keep his distance. He was an illegitimate Texan who fought hard for all he got out of life. Without a golf swing, he was fitted for very little except perhaps a career as a petrol pump attendant.

Nicklaus, on the other hand, had the personal scope to be successful anywhere. Even as an amateur he headed a large insurance business which would have fulfilled most men's lifetime ambition. He had money and he had talent in a greater abundance than perhaps any other man in the history of golf.

Trevino was a disciple of Nicklaus because he acknowledged the man's superiority in skill and technique. This man could win any time he so desired, and Trevino doubted whether there had ever been a golfer of such completeness – not Vardon, Hogan, Snead nor any of them.

Some people suggested that Trevino's clowning was but a defence mechanism against his impoverished background and beginnings, particularly in the highly sensitive and sophisticated world of golf. If it was, then Nicklaus was the man who stopped it. They were chatting in a locker room one day when Nicklaus told Trevino that if he ever discovered just how good he was, the rest of them could pack up and go home. The words remained with Trevino, since they formed the judgement of the man he most respected and since that man never uttered a gratuitous remark about the skill of another player.

For all that respect, Trevino never showed it during the U.S. Open play-off. The professional, anyway, undergoes a transformation when he competes. People lose their indentities and become only faceless opponents. The only purpose in life for a professional is to win, and any obstacle to that aim must be crushed. As Trevino said, there was no such thing for him as a friendly game of golf, and he would not let his wife beat him if he could avoid it.

He also knew that, while he could not catch Nicklaus on a large golf course because of the man's power and the wide range of short-iron clubs it gave him the chance to use, there was a possibility at Merion – a shorter course and claustrophobic enough to inhibit Nicklaus. On this kind of course, the man could be beaten, and that conviction diminished any presence and force of reputation that Nicklaus might bring to the play-off.

Certainly it was Nicklaus who showed signs of strain, particularly with his wedge, where he is considered less than perfect. That club alone was to cost him dearly during the Merion play-off. He had allowed Trevino to get away from him, but at the tenth hole he saw a golden chance of drawing level when a huge drive left him little more than a flick with a wedge from the green.

What emerged would have angered a week-end hacker because the ball was painfully mis-hit and crawled as far as it could towards the green, but was still too far away. Trevino went farther ahead, but while this kind of ill fortune might have been regarded by others as portents of failure, it served only to harden Nicklaus's resolution. He is never more dangerous than when he seems out of the fight, and Trevino knew this. He was like a man with a shark on the end of his fishing line. The fisherman was most vulnerable when the prey suddenly realised that it was fighting for its life. It would be a conflict of will power and stamina, and Trevino still did not consider himself in full command.

On the fourteenth hole, he plunged his approach over the green and a full 6o feet from the flagstick. Hope swelled within Nicklaus, and then died cruelly as Trevino, like an evil magician, coaxed the ball from the trouble and sent it close to the hole.

Nicklaus tried again on the next green, when his own ball lay close to the flag and Trevino was imprisoned in some far-off corner of the green. Trevino glowered as he stalked the ball. He studied it from all angles and, the ritual complete, hunched himself over the ball and eased it into life.

It took an eternity to cover the distance on that green – down little valleys, up and over some hills, skirting the sides of others until it settled on the true course close to the hole that Trevino had perceived. The ball vanished into the hole and there effectively Nicklaus lost the Open and Trevino was champion for the second time.

The triumph brought a deeper confidence to Trevino and at last he could believe what Nicklaus had said about his talent. The saying goes that a lucky man wins the Open once. But only a great man wins it twice. He was now removed from the lucky band of one-timers.

The next week in Cleveland he was so bad that he felt he should not have played. But nobody blamed him for finishing so far down the list. Nicklaus had been smart enough to stay away and prepare for an early trip to Britain for the British Open. Trevino would catch him up later, but there was a lot of ground to cover before that happened.

Trevino, then, could never pass up the chance of playing for money. This attitude was to change, but until that second U.S. Open, he was never sure just how long his period at the top would last, and felt obliged to take what he could find when he could find it. He picked up 750 dollars from Cleveland and there had been times when that was a fortune. Now, after 30,000 dollars from the U.S. Open, it was like loose change.

Anyway, he was committed to play in these events, and there was never time to sit back and enjoy the feeling of being champion. Suddenly it was Montreal and the Canadian Open, and next week it would be Southport, England, and the British Open. Just entries in his diary, another plane, another hotel, another golf course.

Whatever reaction Trevino suffered at Cleveland after his U.S. Open triumph had disappeared by the time he reached the final day of the Canadian Open over the Richelieu Valley course. Art Wall was the leader, but Trevino caught him on the first hole with an iron shot which drilled the ball into the hole for an eagle two.

For the rest of the day these two engaged in a furious battle, each getting the message of the other's blows through distant cheers and snatched glances at the scoreboard. But by late afternoon, it seemed that Wall had prevailed as he stood over a short putt on the last green to take the title.

Trevino, forgetting his rule about smoking cigarettes in

public because of the bad example to children, puffed nervously beside the green. But then a noise in the crowd halted Wall. Some spectators edged forward to get a better view of this man winning. It took a full fifteen minutes to settle them, and all the time Wall stood there looking at his putt. It was a cruel ordeal for a man who had played so gallantly and was losing the battle with himself, and it was made so by the mindless antics of people who should have known better. It cost Wall the Canadian Open, because his putt slithered past the hole.

He knew then that his chance had gone, because a man nearing his fifties can only win by surprise when he catches the others napping. Now he would have to meet Trevino face to face, and he knew it would be a forlorn hope that he could contain this younger man for very long. He was too old for this kind of scrap.

Trevino finished him at the first extra hole with an outrageous putt for a birdie, after Wall had completely lost touch with his surroundings and sent the ball hurtling through the green. The chip back had been brilliantly defiant and clung to the lip of the hole. But Trevino finished him. Exit Art Wall and enter Lee Buck Trevino – U.S. Open and now Canadian Open champion.

Trevino was taken immediately to the airport to catch an overnight flight to Britain, and, by the time that he arrived at Royal Birkdale the following afternoon, everybody had been at work for some time in preparation for the British Open. Only Gary Player and Trevino, both committed to play in Canada, were late-comers.

The Press asked the obvious questions about whether he thought it was too late to prepare himself. He could answer honestly that he knew the course well enough from the 1969 Ryder Cup match; that he had the type of flat punching swing which made transfer to the small ball not quite so difficult; that this kind of swing produced the low-flighted shots which coped adequately with a wind-swept seaside course.

What he could not tell them was that he felt possessed by a perpetual stamina, both mental and physical. It seemed impossible when he thought back over the last three weeks with all its effort and strain. Yet he felt no ill-effects, and those championships, far from draining him, seemed to serve now as proof that he was capable of anything. He knew from his tragedy at St Andrews the previous year that it was possible for him to play well enough on this type of golf course to lead the championship. On that occasion he made the cardinal error of trying to protect his lead and it had all gone wrong. That would not happen again.

Yet, during that championship, the most serious threat to his success came not from the competitors but from the crowd itself. They cheered his errors – and that hurt him deeply.

He was paired in the third round with Jacklin, the people's hero, and it seemed at this stage that the British Open would resolve itself into a duel between these two men. And the crowd left neither in any doubt about which man they wanted to win.

Trevino should have been prepared for it, partly because he knew how important Jacklin was to the British public, and partly because booing was not unknown on this particular course. It was here that the American Ryder Cup team players had some rough treatment from the crowd in 1969.

This time the cheers upset both Jacklin and Trevino because it was an invasion into their private battle, and even though the cheering was short-lived it had a more damaging effect on Jacklin who was embarrassed by this crude display of patriotism.

Even so, the two men engaged in a furious fight down the remaining holes of that round, with Trevino almost inexhaustable as he birdied five of the last seven holes. Jacklin clipped three strokes from the same stretch and, across the horizon came the toothy, hat-doffing Formosan, Lu Liang

Huan, a fragile little man who seemed lost among the towering sandhills of Birkdale.

He was four under par along this stretch, and he acknowledged the delighted roars of the crowd by raising his
hat every time a birdie putt dropped for him. One of these
three men – Trevino, Jacklin or Lu – would be Open champion by the end of the next day.

But somewhere on that final day Jacklin lost his momentum. Perhaps it had really started the night before, when he
implored a reluctant John Jacobs to give him a lesson on
the practice ground. Jacobs knew, as Jacklin did, that this
was no time to be tampering with a swing which, anyway,
had taken him within a stroke of the lead with one round
left to play. Yet if Jacklin's distrust of his swing ran that
deeply, then it was certain to fail him sometime during the
battle of the last day.

So, by the time that Trevino had climbed the sandhill in
pursuit of his errant golf ball on the seventy-first hole, Jacklin
had departed and only Lu retained any interest in the championship . . . and even his had been flagging as Trevino built
a formidable five-stroke lead after a breath-taking burst of
31 strokes over the first nine holes.

The margin had narrowed, but not alarmingly, and even
now as Trevino stood on the hill he tried to convince himself
that whatever this disaster cost him, there would still be
something left to keep clear of Lu. But the next stroke would
change his mind, and offer the Formosan the tantalising
thought that perhaps he himself might become Open champion.

Trevino should have directed himself to getting his ball
back on the fairway. That was of paramount importance,
since only from there could he now produce an effective
scoring stroke and thus offer any defence against Lu. This he
seemed to be doing, until he lashed too hard and rather
blindly with his wedge.

The ball crawled through a spray of sand, and Trevino

fell back and groaned as he realised the ball would not leave the sand bank. It had moved only a few yards. For a moment it looked as if he had lost his temper, for he marched towards the ball, club in hand, as if to chastise the thing. He was almost on the run when he delivered the blow, and this time the ball broke clear . . . but it was going the wrong way, and it soared across the fairway into the rough on the other side.

He was still a long, agonising distance from that green, and in that moment the little Formosan could be forgiven if he cursed his own limitations, for he knew that he could not reach the green with his second and yet that single stroke could close the gap, because Trevino was falling fast. Lu would have to depend on a pitch and a putt, and although Trevino sensed that Lu could not get home with his next blow he watched, with that helpless sinking feeling he had experienced once before at Portland, Oregon, when he had lost a five-stroke lead in three holes to Billy Casper and the then richest prize in the world.

Now it seemed that he was about to hand over an even greater prize to this surprised Oriental who, by any standard, should have been content to finish in the top ten of this exalted company. Lu struck out as hard as he could, but the ball was not strong enough to make the distance and finished short of the green. Trevino, from the clawing rough to which his own anger had condemned him, could only force an iron towards the green and short of the putting surface.

He was helpless, but he was to be saved, not by his own hand but because the man who could have snatched the title from him did not have the depth of experience nor the resources to produce the right stroke at the right time. Lu's admirable finesse which had counteracted his lack of power all week, deserted him when he needed it most. Perhaps he was overwhelmed by the closeness of triumph or surprised by the suddenness with which it had presented itself. He had already lulled himself into a comfortable acceptance of second place, and was totally unprepared for the chance of a better one when it came.

As he stood over the chip shot that needed just to coax the ball close, other forces seemed to numb his hands and mist his accuracy. Trevino again could only watch like a beaten boxer hoping his opponent might suffer muscle cramp in delivering the knock-out blow. But it never came. Lu, unsmiling now, left the ball too far away to be sure. And the putt missed. Once again we had witnessed the truth that winning is always something more than a mathematical count of strokes. There is a gulf which separates the winners from the losers.

For Trevino, the crisis had passed. The hole cost him seven strokes and he held only a one-stroke over Lu as they stood on the final tee. But that was still enough to win, and the thought of it restored his confidence and, as a result, his swing. He won the title.

He had, indeed, captured three major world titles within four weeks, and nobody – not Hogan, Snead, Palmer, Nicklaus nor any of them – had come close to that kind of achievement. It should have been impossible, and yet Trevino had achieved it.

Only on reflection did the enormity of that inspired period take on its proper perspective. Thousands had started the long trail to the U.S. Open. Yet he had triumphed, and in so doing had outplayed, in a head-to-head contest, Nicklaus – the best golfer in the world.

He had mastered whatever was offered in Canada, and he had gone to Birkdale tired and dishevelled, yet again imposed himself on the best players in the world. Some of them took the entire year gathering their form and spirit to a peak for these championships. Trevino had moved through them almost without thinking.

They had been practising at Birkdale long before he arrived. He had to overcome the time change, the lack of practice, the differing conditions. But in those three weeks he established himself as a champion of rare quality; a man with enormous capabilities; a man who could sustain his peak longer than anybody else. He was the only man who could rightfully be ranked alongside Nicklaus. And that meant that there would never again be a need to apologise for being Lee Trevino – the uninvited guest.

Chapter 6: *Tony Jacklin,*
Hazeltine, 1970

He was being compelled, against his will, back to consciousness. He could hear the voice, and for a moment its existence teetered between his dreams and the reality outside his brain. But it tugged persistently and he opened his eyes.

He beheld his infant son, and the sight made Jacklin happy, for no other reason than that the boy was here. But where? His body, lifelessly relaxed, fought his brain, which strove to compute the evidence of the surroundings and stir a memory of how and why he was here.

For precious seconds, the memory refused to work, but then the room, its objects as if hidden by a veil, sprang into its third dimension and a seed of apprehension began to grow within him. He could not recall the reason, but with each second, his awareness became sharper and the feeling was heavier. Then, suddenly, he knew. It came with the realisation of what room this was and what awaited him outside this day. But it was still outside and he was safe here for a moment. His son, secure in his own world and unaware of the ordeal his father faced that day, offered curious comfort.

How sweet to be untouched by all of this; for none of it to matter, and for life's fulfilment to be a full bottle of milk and a dry nappie. By the end of this day, nothing would have changed in that infant's life, and in his son's impregnable world Jacklin found a comforting perspective.

He was leading the U.S. Open on this the final day. At first it had seemed part of the dream. But it was true, even though the reality seemed hard to grasp. His wealth, and the British Open at Lytham, had not made this moment any easier to contemplate. Of course it had always been a dream, but so remote that it was possible to indulge the dream. But not anymore. Now, whatever happened this day, it would never be that kind of dream again.

Winning or losing the U.S. Open would for ever be a patchwork of memories; of putts missed and holed; of sweat and worry; of thousands of people and their noise that was never really heard; of what the others were doing; the panicked glances at the scoreboard; the mystery of a distant roar. These pieces were never parts of his dream, yet today they would become part of his life.

Dare he join Hogan, Jones, Palmer, Nicklaus and Player? And who else? A few years ago he had stood in the crowd of wide-eyed gawpers watching such men pass by. By what right could he now force himself into their company? Sure, the British Open set him on his way. He was a man apart, but it did not put him among the elite. This, now, was a no-man's-land of question marks.

Maybe it had all been too quick and the memories of the ordinary days were still too fresh – fish and chips from newspapers, shared digs because they were cheap, aimless evenings strolling around forgettable towns; the pain of wanting to be known. It was still too razor-sharp to forget, still part of him.

The rest of them were removed, by the passage of time, from these feelings. Player could talk about the days when he trooped round Earls Court looking for somewhere to sleep, but that was now so far away and so removed by his own success that he could have been talking about another man.

A man like Player moves among a small elite, and this atmosphere itself gives evidence, the assurance, of a special place. It is a constant reminder of the superiority of such men – as if they are detached from the rest of the human race. They were, for ever, rare men, and to dream of such a

65

state was easy enough, but the reality much harder to accomplish.

And yet all of them had taken that monstrously arrogant step out of the pack. All of them had broken the shackles and, whatever they became there was for each the moment when they had to take that apparently impossible step. Even the most insensitive of them must have been aware of the enormous presumption and that the task might well be beyond them. However much their egos were sustained in later life by the repetition of such deeds, that first step towards greatness had to be taken against a background of self-doubt.

Now Jacklin, at Hazeltine, had to take that step, or rather the step had presented itself. After three days he had outplayed the world's greatest golfers and stood clear of them.

That in itself was hard to comprehend as he scanned the list and realised that all of them – Nicklaus, Trevino, Casper, Player, Boros, Palmer – were behind him.

Some were to complain that the course was too new and not good enough for the U.S. Open. But it was the same test for everybody, and if there were too many blind holes, too many dog-legs, then everybody had to negotiate them. And if the greens were as treacherous as black ice then everybody faced the same risk of falling on their backsides. Dave Hill could say what he liked and risk the wrath of the American P.G.A. officials, about Hazeltine being short of a herd of cows to complete its usefulness. Jacklin was clear of them all with excellent scores and that was the effective two-fingered answer to all their criticisms.

If they thought this was tough, they ought to tackle a place like Hunstanton on a bleak day with an icy North-Easterly blasting in from The Wash and your whole mind and body shrieking for you to give up and get out of this torment. If you could fight that kind of day, you would never surrender.

Golf was not always a matter of sheer skill. Sometimes the

winning was a test of fortitude and stubborness. That week
Hazeltine demanded it. None of them save Jacklin was prepared to fight the course and in their outraged indignation at
being set such a task it was impossible for them to cope.

It would be a war of attrition, and Jacklin knew how to
fight that kind of warfare from Lytham the year before,
when he had won the British Open. It was impossible not to
become a casualty at some time.

For three days it had been like that at Hazeltine with the
emphasis moving off classical orthodoxy and resting on the
sheer nerve to move the ball forward by whatever means
available. It was a test of invention, where any club in the
bag might be used for a purpose for which it was never
designed.

None of it was so very much different from golf on a foul
English day but it seemed to jar the American players into
protest as if the United States Golf Association could be
blamed for the weather. None seemed able to accept that
what faced them was a test of the ultimate skill in golf – the
ability to make the right judgement without the luxury of
rehearsal. Too many of them were found lacking in this the
essential art.

For Jacklin, it had been instinctive – this ability to take
a punch from the course, shake the head clear, and then
proceed in the knowledge that the time to hit back would
present itself. Once, when he hammered his drive into the
trees, he scrambled after the ball with a seven-iron, grabbed
the club halfway down the shaft and let fly under the trees
so that the ball came out like a supersonic putt and bounced
all the way down the fairway and on to the green to finish by
the hole. That was invention and complete flexibility of
skill. That was the essential golf of Hazeltine that week.

None of this seemed extraordinary to Jacklin, but he was
astounded after that first round to find himself completely
alone at the front of the field and even men such as Nicklaus
languishing ten strokes behind. Indeed, after that first round

Jacklin was to remain alone, uncatchable, in front of the pack which simply could not find its stride.

It was Dave Hill, despite all his costly niggling, who came closest and dogged Jacklin not so much, it seemed, because of his own U.S. Open aspirations, but because he detested the thought of an Englishman getting his hands on the trophy.

He boasted before the third round when they were paired together that he would finish off Jacklin that day, and maybe Hill was still irked by memories of the rough treatment he and Ken Still had received at Birkdale during the 1969 Ryder Cup. All of that had been his own fault. It is always a mistake to take on the crowd.

Whatever the motive, it fired Hill to extreme aggression, but even this offered some help to Jacklin, because at least it localised the threat, even though at times he was more engrossed in redeeming himself from the crises into which his own erratic play had plunged him.

Hill was waiting, like a vulture, for Jacklin to give up the ghost. That would be his moment to swoop, and he thought it had arrived on the twelfth, a gentle dog-leg which trails to the right then shocks the players with a pond tucked near the green.

Jacklin's drive had drifted into a bunker and then, in slight panic, he had made an edgy attempt at distance and the ball clipped the trees, dipped suddenly but found just enough air space to cross the water and reach land on the other side of the pond.

It gave Jacklin precious little room in which to work since he had to get the ball airborne yet halt it close to the hole. But he refused stubbornly to let either Hill's presence or his own sapping memory of what had passed, divert him. The ball was struck close and Hill shrugged and knew he would have to wait a little longer.

The seventeenth should have been the place because Jacklin was unhappy on this hole. On the first day, he had not given the ball enough power to reach the corner for a look at the green and when he had tried to bend his next stroke around the trees, there had been a watery grave for his ball in a pond and a six on his card.

It might have seemed that he got even with the hole the next day, but he was not really convinced since the birdie had been daylight robbery on his part. Once again, the hole had intimidated him into an error and the drive put the ball under a large tree.

A lofted club would send the ball into the branches and anyway would not have enough power to cover the remaining distance to the green. If he took a straight-faced club under the tree, then the ball would have to thread a dangerous path between two ponds which guarded the green.

He reached for a five-iron, grabbed it low, and struck out hard. The ball took off low, racing across the ground, then, like an obedient sheep dog, moved the way its master beckoned between the ponds and up on to the green so close that he birdied the hole. Blind opportunism of course. But Jacklin never questions his luck – good or bad.

On the third day he came again to the seventeenth and, pestered by memories, swung without sufficient confidence at the ball and paid the penalty of a hurried incomplete swing. The ball plunged into deep rough on the left behind the trees.

He had no view of the green and no apparent line of attack. No straight-faced club could bore a route through that clustered foliage. Hill had been waiting for such a moment, and it angered Jacklin to think that he had given it to this American.

Yet he would not – could not – yield now because, if this was to be his week, the week when the gods gave him their approval, then there was only one possible way to find out. He had to attack and attempt, if not the impossible, then at least the audacious. Anyway it was marginally better than meek surrender, because even if he did lose this week, he could not live with the suspicion that he had not taken all his chances.

He reached for his eight-iron with the obvious intent of gaining sufficient height to clear the top of the trees. But that was only part of the job. Then the ball would have to find the power to cover 150 yards to the green. It was much to ask but at least it would settle, in his own mind, the question of whether he was simply dabbling, by sheer chance, at the front of this distinguished field, or whether destiny had marked him down for this title.

He lashed savagely at the ball. Within a second he knew that it was clear – then he was running forward to the brow of the hill to see if it was strong enough to get home.

But before he could see for himself, he heard the roar of the crowds which told him and Hill that the ball was on the green. Jacklin was still alone at the end of the day, and went away that night with a four-stroke lead.

Now, the final act. The night before, his legs had been tormented by paralysing cramps and he had wrapped them in linament, so that by morning the pain had eased somewhat. A sleeping pill had taken him quickly into healing unconsciousness until his son awoke him. But there was another problem to be faced : how should he spend the endless dragging hours until he was required on the first tee? He could not afford to be distracted totally from the task ahead because that would dissipate his gathering mood. Neither could he sit there and dwell on the possibilities.

He needed to be dulled just a little so that his imagination lost its edge. He took half a sleeping pill to help him through the hours that remained before he was due at the course. Then he waited, at first easing his legs in a bath, then talking to friends although removed a little by the drug so that at times he could hear his voice as though it came from someone else.

Then it was time to go, and Jacklin felt relief and reluctance as time bore him inevitably towards a conclusion he was afraid to discover. When he reached the locker and opened the door, he was puzzled by a note inside. It contained one word : 'TEMPO'.

He guessed that Yancey or Weiskopf wrote it. They knew his constant weakness was this impetuosity which sometimes fired his swing into uncontrollable action. He resolved to cling to that thought for the rest of the day.

Then he warmed as he realised the note offered more than technical assistance. It showed that somebody else cared; that these two men were happy enough in his good fortune to urge him to a title both would dearly have loved themselves.

It was a small gesture but, to Jacklin, enormous encouragement. These had been three of the loneliest days of his life and now he realised that he was not alone. It was as though the kaleidoscope had been jolted and the pattern changed to give more shape. And that was all he needed.

The afternoon began sensibly enough and Jacklin was launched well into his round before he realised that it was all going smoothly and yet he felt it was all too quiet to last. He breathed a little easier, even though there was no reason to, because, as much as anybody in that field, he knew it was impossible to walk through Hazeltine unscathed. His turn would come.

Before he knew it, the crisis was upon him, starting innocently enough with the merest fraction of error. The words of Yancey and Weiskopf had been forgotten in his irritation at a missed birdie putt, and he swung vengefully at his drive from the seventh tee and the ball fizzed crazily out of control into the trees some yards ahead of him and an appalling distance from the green.

He laboured miserably through it in six strokes and suddenly he was mentally off-balance as though he had mislaid his campaign plans. His touch became unsure, and from the next tee he overwhelmed the ball with unwanted strength and put it in trouble behind the green. And, once again, his powers of recovery could not save him.

Hill, now playing ahead of him, was still the menace, and Jacklin by his own errors had allowed the American to creep within three strokes. Yet, if the title was beginning to move away Jacklin did not notice it, as he became more engrossed in the immediate matters of restoring his composure and finding what the hell was going wrong. Anyway, he could face only one stroke at a time and the wider implications would have to wait.

That had always been the same, whether winning the Lincolnshire amateur or the Holme Hall monthly medal, or here now with the U.S. Open championship. The outcome could wait, and anyway was totally irrelevant somehow to the problems which faced him between here and the clubhouse. Perhaps this was the drug of winning. The fruits were acceptable, but it was the process of winning, the act itself which held more lure. Afterwards the two were indivisible but they had a merciful separation during the height of the conflict.

But still the swing had not settled by the time he struck his drive from the ninth tee, and the ball drilled like a bullet into long grass beside the fairway. He pounced, almost angrily, and lashed the ball towards the green as if punishing it for his troubles. And when he reached the green, the defiant ball was still a long way from the flagstick.

Jacklin, his face tight with strain and a hint of exasperation, struck out much too hard with his putter and the ball, like a frightened dog escaping a beating, took off fast. The spectators were horrified, looked quickly beyond the flagstick to see how much green was available on the other side, and tried to guess whether the putt would stay on.

But whatever else, Jacklin had judged the line perfectly. The ball sped towards the hole and, as it was about to pass, suddenly realised that this was home. It hit the back of the hole and jumped in the air. Then, still defiant, it perched on the edge. For a moment it looked as though ball and man were staring each other out. But the cold look of fury hardened in Jacklin's eyes and it was too much for the ball, which cowered into the hole. Jacklin was still the master.

That was the birdie that restored Jacklin and that was the moment he won the U.S. Open. That improbable birdie, fashioned in abject despair, not only enlarged his lead but also told him this was to be *his* championship. He was U.S. Open champion by seven strokes.

Now it would all start – the other part of winning. A million dollars? The saviour of British golf? Palmer, Nicklaus, Player, Jones, Hagen, Snead, Trevino and now Jacko – Bill Shakland's assistant – the lodger from Potters Bar. Thousands had started out towards this title. Now there was only him left.

There was still no time to comprehend it as he trotted out the answers that the Press wanted to hear. He spoke to them with another part of his mind and as if not yet catching up with reality. For his son, it was a day like any other. A full bottle of milk and a dry backside. What more could anybody ask?

Chapter 7: *Gary Player, Wentworth, 1965*

In Johannesburg, his father waited by the radio for news and, when it came, it was bad. Gary was taking a beating. It was more than simple defeat. What was happening there at Wentworth was much worse. It was total humiliation, a gigantic come-uppance in front of a crowd that didn't much care and perhaps secretly savoured the enormity of this collapse. Even Lema, the man who was ruining him, felt moved to apologise as best he could for the way it was going.

The feelings of the crowd did not touch Player. If he could not inspire the kind of affection that De Vicenzo or Palmer enjoyed, then at least they had respect for his reputation. But in that moment he knew that nobody, apart from his wife and his caddie, really cared or was touched by the sight of a man who had pursued success all his life suddenly coming face-to-face with the worst kind of failure.

Perhaps his unabashed ambition in those days eliminated any chance of deep affection from the public. He had burned inside with the obsession to be good. It began as a dream, then became so fixed that his life was given over to it. Yet because his evolution had been so public – because they had seen the raw material and now the finished product – he seemed but a montage of acquired ability and somehow less gifted, less worthy, because of it.

It was a wrong judgement, but it existed. He was so apparently self-made. He had built up his muscles and overcome his unorthodoxy by ruthless hard work. And the judgement was wrong because who is not self-made? Who has not developed, experimented and evolved a skill and ability to win? No golfer, save perhaps Nicklaus, was born gifted.

Indeed, Player's deficiences had much to do with his strength of character which became so vital to his winning. His compulsion to overcome them drove him to endless effort, and this itself became part of his style. Whenever Player won, he was manifestly trying harder than anybody else. Perhaps that show of determination belied the outstanding skill on which it was based.

In the early years, he always returned to Johannesburg from his world travels having learned something from a good golfer. He would, for example, seek out the best wedge player and watch him at work for hours until the snooping became irritating. But he would watch long enough to copy, then work alone until he got it right.

What gave him that determination? The pioneer strain was in him and the rest of his family, but none had shown the same compelling drive. Maybe it was the need for purpose that gave him purpose. He believed that something was waiting for him somewhere in his life. It was a faith, a monumental presumption, but it was enough to give purpose to the meantime and force him to pursue excellence beyond the point when good sense demanded some respite.

In the beginning, his golf and the hours spent hitting a golf ball had been a way to pass the time. There was nothing else. But gradually it became an inflexible routine and nobody quite remembered when it happened. Suddenly it was more than boyish enthusiasm which drove Gary to golf. Absolute dedication, of course. But to him, it was more — his end of the bargain with fate. A preparation for a destiny already expected, if not defined.

But the dangers of simple conviction is that nobody else believes it without evidence. Player could never be a truly private person, and his outward honesty sounded very much like boasting. His early days in Britain had been rough for him since he had no protective shell, and there is something in the British character which distrusts overt ambition in a man. The seasoned professionals were maliciously cruel to him, and he was surprised and hurt by their reaction. He had expected help and enthusiasm, and if such an attitude was grossly naïve then it demonstrated his enormous ignorance of human nature. And yet it was a great blessing, since this experience not only strengthened his resolve but also compelled him to acquire the hard shell of self-sufficiency which he had lacked.

He realised, then, that he had to be impregnable, and that his concentration had to acquire a myopic focus on the job in hand. Throughout his life he was to demonstrate this mystic ability to remove himself from his surroundings and concentrate on his task. The time would come when his life was threatened, when he would play golf flanked by armed guards. But never once did he mention it as an excuse. Never once did it deter him from playing his best.

Player had the will to win long before he had the means, and this curious balance drove him to extremes of dedication which perhaps only the monkish Hogan surpassed. The more fierce his determination, the more harshly he judged himself and the higher standard he expected and achieved. The end-product was a unit of skill and character more formidable than any other around him.

But on that day, at Wentworth, against Lema, he was being driven to the nightmarish conclusion that all of it – every ball struck, his ambition, dedication, devotion and even God's will – was not enough. It was in its way, a crisis of faith, since he had never doubted that it was the Almighty directing his path through life.

It might seem an overstatement, but the professional golfer's justification for his existence is the constant demonstration of his superiority. The money helps, but it is the addictive quality of winning which lures men.

Nothing is more important. When a three-foot putt is less important than the world's starving children and other injustices, then the professional is finished. When he can put his

Arnold Palmer hits clear from a 20 ft. high sand hill on the
way to the eighth green at Royal Birkdale.

Jack Nicklaus leaps high after making the winning putt at St Andrews.

– and his countryman Doug Sanders ducks the putter which the exuberant Nicklaus has thrown into the air.

A large crowd watch as Ben Hogan drives from the tenth at
Carnoustie.

Above: Jacklin throws his ball to the crowd after holing his final putt at Royal Lytham and St Annes. *Below:* Trevino went on to win – after falling on his knees when holing a long putt on the eighth green.

A birdie putt on the eighteenth green – and Jacklin is the
first Englishman in fifty years to win the U.S. Open.

Above: De Vicenzo chips on the eleventh green at Hoylake. He shot a final round of 70 for a total of 278. *Below:* Blasting from a bunker on the second in his final round.

Peter Thomson, the new Open Champion, followed by ex-
Champion Tony Lema, with their caddies on the eighteenth
at Royal Birkdale after the final hole.

Left: A grimace, as Trevino misses a putt on the sixth green during the first round of the 1972 Open.

Right: And a gesture of defeat at the tenth when he thought that the Championship was lost.

Left: Champion after all, Trevino walks off the course with the vanquished Tony Jacklin.

game into perspective, he is ruined. That is perhaps the sadness of professional sport – its callous self-importance.

Yet, although Player knew how important it was, that day at Wentworth, there was nothing that he could do. Lema had him on the floor and was losing interest. Even the crowd was bored by it and walked away. His emotions were confused, his thoughts crazily kaleidoscoped. His own task was hard enough against the course and all the time Lema was stabbing at him as well. There was the sudden panic of realisation that he might be deprived of the most important thing in his life at the moment – a triumph.

He reached the depth of despair and felt hollow, transparent as though he did not exist. The next thought in his mind must be to accept without question that he was going to lose. But it was not. The thoughts were changing, but something curious was happening. He could not believe it as the gnawing emptiness within him was suddenly filled with unwarranted strength and confidence. He was puzzled, like a man scrambling to make sense of those last seconds before he submerges under an anaesthetic. It possessed him completely. From that moment – until he collapsed in tears when it was all over – he was caught up, blanketed, by a spiritual force which he could never explain.

Lema still leaned comfortably on a five-hole lead as they prepared to play the last nine holes of this semi-final in the Piccadilly World Match Play. He knew that there was enough in the bank to see him comfortably through since he had only to match Player over the remaining holes, and even if he failed here and there, his credit must be good enough. He might lose a few, but there would always be enough left.

He lost the short tenth over the trees with a vexing iron shot which missed the green. Player knifed into a drive on the next tee and drilled the ball down the valley and up the other side, and emerged with a birdie. Now Lema had lost two holes and, strangely, that thought impinged more on him than the positive aspect that he was still three up with six to play.

Already tension had replaced his quiet assurance and already he could feel the first stirrings of the battle within himself. Now they were watching him for mistakes. Now the question was whether he, Lema, could hold on to what he possessed? Would he give it back, or could Player snatch it?

In the midst of this inward battle, he struck out with his driver on the thirteenth hole where the fairway cuts round the dense jungle on the left towards the green at the foot of the hill. The action was all wrong, his body in the wrong place, but he was powerless to halt the momentum that would bring disaster. The ball snapped angrily left, heading low and hard for the jungle.

Player's ball offered goading insult as it nestled in the middle of the fairway, and Lema knew that very soon there might be nothing left to protect. He must now fight all the way home. He looked down sadly at his ball trapped in the trees, flailed blindly through grass and twigs, and the ball resentfully moved forward a few yards. Player was already standing over his ball. But he waited because he wanted Lema to see this one. Then he cracked down hard and the cheers seconds later told them both it was a perfect stroke.

Lema's purpose was now withering. He pitched towards the green and the ball, in another act of treachery, stopped a long way from the hole. Player waited for him to putt, practising his own stroke and gazing unconcernedly around the countryside. If he showed disinterest now, Lema knew that Player would watch that ball every inch of the way to the hole. Perhaps Lema could hole it. What a tremendous blow that would be. Daylight robbery to be sure, but maybe just enough to unsettle Player (and slip in, winning the hole with his own putt).

Lema was too far from the hole to calculate seriously or worry overmuch about the borrows. He struck, and both men watched the ball gather the distance to the hole, then, with its last gasp, disappear. Lema sighed with relief convinced that he had saved himself. The length of that putt and the contrasting manner each man had played the hole must now add intolerable pressure to Player's own putt.

Player felt it. His path to the hole was a tortuous curve to the right, but how far left should he direct the ball to allow it to find its own way home? If he missed it would restore Lema's flagging confidence.

His preparations were complete. He could look at the line for another thousand years and learn no more about it. Now he must strike. It was a moment of awful irrevocability. He was standing safely on one side of the barrier between present and future. But there, ten feet away, was the future which had to be met. He struck, and the ball trickled slowly into the hole.

Now Lema had only two left, and he could take no comfort from the thought, because he was oppressed not only by Player's retaliation but also by the sudden realisation that his own game was going to pieces. At the back of it all was the memory of that last green. If you hole a 25-foot putt and still lose the hole, it is not going to be your day.

Lema's blind instinct for survival kept Player at bay for another two holes and he tried to think only that, with three left to play, he needed only to halve a couple of them – not win, just halve. Just match this little fellow, stroke for stroke. Anyway, Player would not take chances with the sixteenth, not with all those trees pressing from both sides and he certainly had no advantage over the long finishing holes.

But Player had other ideas. He reached for his driver on that sixteenth tee and made sure that Lema noticed. Both had left this club in the bag during the morning because the margin for error was too fine. But now Player wanted to frighten Lema perhaps into another error. Lema had already shown he was suspect with the driver. Could Player now lure him into another irrational stroke? He drilled his own ball perfectly into the fairway, and waited.

Lema was painfully confused because he daren't go with his driver, but nor could he allow Player too much advantage of a short and more accurate iron into that green. There were too many contradictions, too many worries, in the American's mind when he let fly with his three-wood, and all of them showed in the stroke. Once again the ball fizzed on a suicide course to the left and Player's gamble had paid off. Lema was only one up with two to play.

He had to believe, but could not, that it was still enough. The comfort of statistics had been smothered by a more overpowering mood, in which he was already losing, and Player winning. The walk from the seventeenth tee down the hill and round the corner to the green passed for both of them in an instant. Suddenly they were looking at their putts, and Lema was first to play.

Lema could think of nothing now except that this ball must drop. He could still finish Player here. The mind was blank and the body took command and drilled the ball into the hole. Now Player was the man with all his options gone. Now he was compelled to one act – the only act that would save him.

Not that the thought, in such precise terms, occurred to him. Like Lema, he was caught up in the possessing urgency to direct this ball into the hole. The act seemed to matter more than the consequences, and maybe if he had missed, he would have needed somebody to tell him what it meant. But he holed it, and Lema, clinging to one hole, stood on the last tee, forcing himself to remember that it could all finish in a few minutes.

If this was ordeal by fire, then at least he could see where the flames ended. If he could keep this persistent man at arm's length for the next quarter of a mile, it was all over. That now mattered more than the implications of winning – a place in the final. That had been forgotten.

But Lema could not shake off the awful horror of how this disaster had ambushed him. At least Player had lived with the prospect of failure all day. But it had happened too quickly for Lema, who could not rationalise the changing pattern – nor step away from it for a moment – to restore his composure. After all, he had led and was still leading. Why, then, did he feel like a loser?

Both men carefully put their tee shots into play and far enough up the fairway to see the green around the corner of the trees. But no matter how manfully Lema struggled, his resilience had snapped and his effort was all but spent. His next stroke dribbled meekly short of the green, and Player knew that this was to be the moment.

But when he struck the ball, he thought he was ruined. He had wanted to reach the green, more so now, because Lema had failed. But the ball raced towards the trees on the right, and for a sickening moment, as it disappeared from view, he was certain it would be brought down. But the noise of collision did not come, and he realised that it must have found a way through. Then came the cheer, and its intensity told him that the crowds by the green were looking at something very good. The ball had curved away from the trees in an obedient arc, and skipped past a bunker to finish close to the flagstick.

Lema was so shattered that his basic professionalism began to desert him. The tension was too stifling to make objective observations. He forgot that the greens would be slowed by a covering of dew and that he would need to strike his pitch shot much harder. The ball halted yards from the hole, and this time there was to be no life-saving putt. They were all square on the last green and were now compelled to play extra holes.

Player had shaken off a five-hole deficit and knew that no matter how many extra holes it took, Lema was going to lose. Instinctively, Lema launched himself at his drive on the first extra hole – but he couldn't overtake Player's ball.

The memory of what he had lost and perhaps the thought of starting again, now suffocated him. He was never mentally prepared to hit that long approach across the valley to the green, and the ball snaked low and plunged into a bunker below the green.

It was there for Player to take – just one stroke across that valley. Even before he picked up its flight, the sweet explosion in his arms told Player that he had made good contact with the ball. He was home, and that mattered most. Lema, like a sleep-walker, went through the motions – a bunker shot to a 'phantom' pin yards away from the real one, and a putt that missed the hole. He stood back and waited, like a condemned man praying in those last precious seconds that the trap-door would fail to open – yet knowing that it would. Player finished it there.

He shook hands with Lema, although neither was aware of his surroundings. Player's wife rushed forward, and they began to walk back down the fairway to the clubhouse. Then, suddenly, the world went grey. Player weakened and flopped to the ground. He was crying, although he did not know the reason. He passed out and trembled. A doctor in the crowd rushed to help him. In moments, he was better.

That night he could not sleep but at least the agony, for him, was over. But until the day he died, Lema would sometimes wake up in the middle of the night wondering just what went wrong that day at Wentworth.

Chapter 8: *Roberto De Vicenzo,*
Hoylake, 1967

De Vicenzo felt he must run to his hotel room because he knew that he was about to cry and that he must hide. Yet he forced himself to walk at measured pace which gave the outward appearance that he had not lost his perpetual serenity. The walk from the last green at Carnoustie to the Bruce Hotel takes less than four minutes and he smiled, nodded and shrugged at well-wishers until he disappeared through the hotel lobby and walked upstairs. Then, when he had closed the bedroom door, he cried.

With one round of that 1953 British Open to be played that afternoon he shared the lead with Hogan, but he knew in his bones that he could not win. It was not Hogan and his declared appointment with destiny that afternoon that convinced De Vicenzo, but rather some blinding and unwanted revelation which told him that the afternoon would be no different from the morning. His putting was hopeless and it would not change.

He cried not so much because he was going to lose, but because this was the frustration of his life – a peerless talent that was destroyed by his temperament; by this perception that could see such portents and make them a reality; by a mind that was acutely aware to every damnable pressure.

All his life he had followed a punishing practice routine in the manner of a concert pianist, keeping his technique proficient by daily practice – four hours hitting balls and then a round of golf. But none of it could give him the essential deafness and blindness with which the champion protects himself from outside torments.

That day at Carnoustie the technique had worked effic-
iently, and certainly no less than the legendary robot manner
of Hogan. But on those greens De Vicenzo had been bewildered, and was like a bullfighter who had manoeuvred the
bull into submission and then realised that he had come without his sword. He lost.

Once again he had more evidence of a truth too awful to
accept – that he did not have the temperament to win a
major title. Of course, he had won a lot of things, but they
were little and didn't matter. It made him squirm uncom-
fortably when they announced on the first tee of a tournament just how many Open titles he had won. They were all
little Opens in backwaters of the world where nobody but he
ventured. That, at least, is how he felt. If he had won that
many events, then he could not forget that few of the really
big men had ever turned up to challenge him. Nobody had
travelled more extensively in pursuit of a major title and even
if he collected the little ones, he never ducked the big ones,
either.

He was, nevertheless, a reluctant traveller, forced by the
demands of his chosen profession to put thousands of miles
between himself and his family. He had been around the
world at least 35 times, and it never became easier to separate
himself from his loved ones. As the day for departure approached he would try to find all manner of reasons why he
should not get the suitcase from the cupboard, pack the
clothes, and kiss the family farewell.

Perhaps this, too, was part of the reason why he did not
show the essential self-sufficiency that makes a champion;
that he was never able to think only of himself but was painfully aware of the sacrifices his sons and his wife were making
by his absence in pursuit of his goal. All of it conspired to
make his efforts seem half-hearted, and that afternoon De
Vicenzo at Carnoustie lost, as he knew he would.

The years passed, and it became a sad, but bearable,
fact of his life that he could make an excellent living which

gave his family the wealth of several businesses in Buenos Aires, even if he could not capture a major world title. His routine into early middle-age followed its predictable pattern of wrenching farewells, exhausting travel, ordinary triumphs and a thickening bank account.

He could list 130 tournament victories around the world and these included 30 national championships, but he would have traded the lot for just one big victory – the British, the U.S., or the Masters. It could be just a cruel quirk of fate, since other people were not frequent winners, but when they did triumph it was invariably in a big event. Julius Boros was a case in point. De Vicenzo could win more often – but never the ones he really wanted.

However, he never relinquished the hope that the pattern might change. He could not, because the entire point of his existence would have finished. But when he reached the age of 45, he knew that time was running out. He came to Hoylake in 1967 more in hope than intent.

His philosophy then was: 'Anytime your mind wanna play, you can win. But if your mind don't wanna play, then you're dead. In this game your have the chance to play any time your mind says so. I never think I am the man to win. I have too much respect for the other players to think that. Always, I play for position. If it's good after three rounds, then maybe there is chance to win.'

But it was becoming increasingly difficult to force his mind to play, and he joked with people that he came to Britain only to see his old friends, and he gave the same excuse when he visited the United States where his equally long pilgrimage had yielded more cash than glory.

His arrival at the Royal Liverpool clubhouse in that summer of '67 was unobtrusive, and altogether different from the grey-flannelled reception committee that awaited the star, Jack Nicklaus. When Nicklaus's limousine swept into the car park, the word spread like a bush fire around the course, and people came just to see the defending champion supervise the unloading of his clubs and kit from the car.

De Vicenzo could never emote that kind of appeal, since he was the old campaigner and so much part of the furniture that nobody ever bothered about him. You could walk into a bar, then realise after ten minutes that you had been sitting next to him all that time. Nicklaus, on the other hand, had star appeal, and moved constantly amid a cloud of hangers-on, and yet bore it all with the tolerance of a horse on a summer's day who knows there is no way of out-running the flies.

Even though Nicklaus and the others were to dominate the headlines during the preceding days of the championships De Vicenzo had gathered immense confidence, and if he was a man who looked for and accepted portents then there were enough around beforehand to comfort him. He had beaten Nicklaus in a prolonged T.V. match, and while this held no material significance, such are the interminable delays between shots, at least he could remember that he had maintained his concentration through it all with a greater persistence than Nicklaus. Then, on the Sunday, De Vicenzo had won the Roosevelt Nine Nations tournament, a one-day charity match in aid of crippled children.

All of it told him that his swing was working with fluid efficiency and that, more importantly, his mind wanted to play golf. He had another strength, born of his previous failure, because he had been too close to the title too often to be frightened by it and at worst he knew that failure was not so terrible and that he could live with it. That thought alone would allow him to play more freely and without the inhibitions of a man who senses that it is in his stars to win, sometime.

He needed two things – a reasonable share of holed putts, those middle-distance terrors that earn birdies but, more importantly, save pars when things go awry. And he needed luck. Nobody wins anything without luck.

Luck is an indefinable, yet glaringly apparent, part of any

golfer's success. One can argue that the best players emerge on top too often to rely on luck; that they make their own luck, yet one can see them play and, in the process of winning, see evidence of enormous good fortune.

Trevino's shot from the bunker into the sixteenth hole, during the third round of the 1972 British Open at Muirfield, was an awful stroke. Yet the ball caught the flagstick and ran down into the hole, thus materially affecting the outcome of that championship. The next day, on the seventy-first hole, when Trevino was convinced he had thrown the title away, he chipped carelessly and the ball ran into the hole and so doing won him the championship. Was it luck? What is luck? Is it always in the eye of the beholder – and the loser?

Whatever it was, De Vicenzo wanted his share of it, because he knew that he would have to work hard on every stroke over that golf course for four days, and for him it would be, as he approached middle age, a longer and more difficult fight. The others might have more chances in future years, but he felt that he would never feel this good again at the start of a championship. In fact, however, he did a year later, when his score tied the U.S. Masters at Augusta Georgia, but he was deprived of the chance of a play-off because of a mistake on his scorecard which he failed to spot. For ever afterwards he claimed the U.S. Masters as one of his triumphs, although Bob Goalby was given the winner's green jacket, because 'nobody beat my score for that championship'.

But there at Hoylake he suspected that he faced his last chance, and he prayed that, if there were to be bad strokes, they would not be disastrous. Even so, he was confident enough to tell his friends with whom he stayed, close to the course : 'This year, I have good chance.'

Hoylake suited him because its narrow fairways peppered with bunkers and buffeted by wind demanded a crucial accuracy that could come only from clean striking, and De

Vicenzo's life since he had turned professional had been given over to the acquisition and retention of that art. He also had the experience to cope with any kind of capricious wind that plagued the British seaside. But he prayed that it would not rain, because this bothered him greatly and he could not see well enough in the rain to judge distances.

It was a serious deficiency to take into a championship, and he started on the first day with a 33–1 chance according to the bookmakers. He ploughed an unobtrusive, yet competent, furrow for two days, leaving the sensations to others. Nicklaus shared the halfway lead with Devlin, the Australian, and De Vicenzo was one stroke behind.

On that second night, a violent thunderstorm ravaged the course and it woke De Vicenzo, who prayed that the rain would stop by the time he had to play. It did, and in fact became part of the luck he needed. The rain had tamed this fast-running course to give him immeasurable confidence as he tackled it in the third round.

He cut loose with uncharacteristic savagery and pieced together a 67 which equalled the course record set an hour earlier by Gary Player who stayed two strokes behind the new leader De Vicenzo with one round of the championship to be played.

De Vicenzo had played for position all his life and now he was clear of everybody. But this itself was a problem, because he was confused about his next strategy. Should he attack to try to open a bigger lead but at the same time run the risk of finding trouble that would harm him? And how would he feel at the end of the day if he had taken these chances then realised they were not necessary and that somebody else had won the title because of his errors? And yet surely one of them, Nicklaus or Player, would make a charge. One of them would break loose. It had been easier when somebody else was in front. But when you have to call the tune...

He slept badly that night, and was in a highly nervous

state when he reached the first tee for the final round. Player, his partner, was already waiting and anxious to get into the scrap. De Vicenzo caught sight of Player standing there, and suddenly he was struck by a curious and uplifting thought as if seeing the South African for the first time : 'He looked so small and weak. So little. I say to myself what the hell? You can't be afraid of this little fellow?

So it began, an afternoon of intense conflict with De Vicenzo, in this mood, prevailing over Player then withstanding a furious onslaught from Nicklaus. It took De Vicenzo twelve holes before he could shake off Player, and only then because of what he called the essential luck of a winner.

Both played errant tee shots to this short hole which runs along the shore. From the tee, it looked as if both had been struck on the same suicidal path and neither stroke was worse than the other. Yet when De Vicenzo found his ball, the lie was good enough for him to reach the green and salvage a par three. Player was not so fortunate, and could not rescue his ball from the suffocating long grass to match the Argentinian. Two equally bad strokes had been played but with such differing results.

Even with Player out of the way, De Vicenzo knew it was not over because the roars from the crowds ahead told him that Nicklaus was pressing hard. And yet the Argentinian displayed a serenity which made us all think that somehow he had seen the last page of this drama and knew the outcome.

He showed it in so many ways. On the long sixteenth hole, he drove contemptuously close to the out of bounds zone which bites into the fairway from the right, then drilled his three-wood, with a gentleness that belied its fury, into the faraway green.

Nicklaus was playing well but too late, and the birdie putt he sank on the last green was a despairing gesture because he sensed it was not enough to intimidate De Vicenzo, nor deflect him from his purpose. Par golf over the last two holes would see De Vicenzo as British Open champion and, as he came safely through the seventeenth, a thousand prayers from those spectators wafted heavenwards that nothing should go wrong now for Roberto.

He drove, then the crowd erupted into ecstatic relief as his approach shot found the safety of that last green. Long before he reached there, they were cheering wildly, and he removed his cap hesistantly to acknowledge their happiness. It is doubtful whether any triumph – perhaps even Jacklin's, subsequently, at Lytham – earned the unrestrained and tearful joy that greeted Roberto's triumph that day.

Jacklin, Nicklaus and the rest of them might do it again. But not this man, and for all of us who stood there, blinking back the tears in that highly emotional moment, it was a rare privilege to be present at the precise point in time when a man's lifetime of work is rewarded. He had earned those tears and the cheers by a lifetime of persistence.

It was all over quickly, and two putts later he was champion. Later that evening I had finished my story and was walking through the gathering gloom to the car park. They had all gone home, the champions departed. But then I saw a crowd of people. In the middle of them, the big man was still signing autographs.

He looked up and saw me. He looked tired and trapped and he said : 'Take me away from this. I'm tired.' I shook my head and said : 'I can't do that Roberto. These people have waited twenty years for this to happen.' He shrugged and carried on signing.

Chapter 9: *Peter Thomson, Royal Birkdale, 1965*

Thomson was in his hotel room, not sure whether anybody downstairs had noticed that he was absent, but not really bothered since he was here by choice. It was too easy to get involved, to waste the hours talking of golf and, more important to become distracted from the purpose which brought him here to Birkdale. He needed to keep that thought in his mind more than he needed their company.

Winning had become more difficult – not just because the competition was keener now, but also because he was getting older and knew how his temperament and concentration, which had coped with it all at one time, now had to be nursed to function properly.

This aloofness suited his mood and reflected the changes within the game that had pushed him into the background. He was, after all, the forgotten man, overtaken by the giant-sized impact of the Palmer era and all that followed in its wake. It had been six years since he had won the title, and in that time the emphasis had changed because now winning was, of itself, not enough. It had to be accompanied by a charisma, a public appeal that lifted the winner from his customary role of craftsman into the hysterical world of public entertainer.

So great had this change become that he was already but a name in the record books, and his achievements as far removed for the current mood as the exploits of young Tom Morris.

Even that might have been bearable except that now his achievements were being questioned as to just how many of those four British Opens he would have won had there been any world-class talent against him. It hurt to think that what had been joyfully accepted at the time was now being cheapened by hindsight.

What damned him, of course, was his lack of success in the United States, the acknowledged arena, and his genuine dislike for that way of life had always been taken as a pretty thin excuse for a lack of comprehensive skill to cope with their playing conditions.

In fact the parallel with young Tom Morris was not that far removed in their minds since Thomson seemed to belong to the hit-and-hope era where caution and an ability to bumble along had won titles. Such primitive strategy had now been replaced by a precision play where men consulted note-books, rather than trust their eyes, to make decisions on a golf course. This was precision play, the new golf, and Thomson epitomised the old type.

To him there was only one sort of golf, and it had not changed in its essential demands of skill and judgement since the days of the Morrises and the Kirkaldys. Golf was the ability to control a golf ball over a stretch of terrain that had been left as the Almighty had made it. If that meant awkward bounces, unjust patches of rough and greens as receptive as concrete, then it was no reason why skills could not be developed, as they had always been, to cope.

In any case, there was a safe way around every course, no matter how tough and impossible it might at first appear. The correct stroke, positioned in the right place, was never subject to these unfair bounces or quirks of fate.

Any golfer worthy of the name soon gets the feel of a golf course, and the better he learns, the more qualified he is for the rewards. The taming of golf courses, through watered greens and tailored rough, had dispensed with that benefit.

And yet none of this could be offered as a reason for his paltry recent efforts in the British Open, which of all the championships, remained closest to the original conditions of play and its philosophies. It was six years since he had last won the title.

Each year he had directed himself towards the British Open, and everything he did, every tournament he played, was part of this preparatory process. He might be in Hong Kong, yet he would experiment with a driver that could work well for him at the British Open and on the particular course where it would be played.

Because he had won he knew precisely what was involved in the process, and knew through the intervening years whether or not he was ready, fully equipped to take the title. Not once in that time had he really thought he was ready.

What *does* it take? Perhaps only eight men ever come to any Open fully prepared in every department to win. The rest are just hopeful also-rans playing for the prize money. Some of them might be dragged to a standard beyond themselves, but they never win.

The winning of a championship is based on near-faultless golf. It is possible to win a championship with at most two errors a round. The way the Open championship courses are styled allows a man no more than two errors if he is to stay with the leading pace. Then again, nobody prevents a man winning the Open. It is his own bad strokes which ruin him.

Thus if the man is operating at his best standard when he arrives, it is the elimination of the poor strokes that will win the title for him. That, at least, was the thinking process for Thomson. He also knew that anybody who had a serious doubt about part of his own game, could not win, because some time during the four rounds that weakness would find him out. No matter how many times a man might hole outlandish putts and scramble his pars, if there was a weakness it would ruin him. Thus very few men ever came to the British Open in the comforting knowledge that their game was at its peak.

But that year at Birkdale, everything had come together in Thomson's favour. His own golf was as good as it had ever been, the preparatory process had been perfectly timed to bring him to his peak that week. The pollen count was low so that his hay fever was a minor problem. But most of all, Birkdale was hard and fast. It was made for him, and if he could not hit the ball as far as the real power merchants, then this week it would be his greatest asset, because their ability to cart the golf ball huge distances could bring only disaster. This week the ball had to be kept on a tight rein and never once get away from its master.

Despite his growing confidence, he remained very much a supporting act in the pre-championship circuit where headlines were swallowed by Palmer and Nicklaus and Player, and the customary breathless last-minute arrival of Tony Lema the defending champion.

Thomson did not mind, and rather preferred it, because now he had to protect and nurture his thinking process. He knew that it would require nerve to win, that at some time he would be confronted by a crisis which, if he handled it properly, would be the last obstacle between himself and the championship.

Hence he wished to be left alone to spend the evenings in his hotel, eating in his room, away from talk of golf and the oppressing mood of the championship, and listening instead to the radio and classical music. In any case, winning was the last stage – an opportunity which presented itself only after three rounds of diligence. His first task was to put himself close enough to the front to have this winning chance.

It was a conditioning process in which he discouraged outward contact. When his practice was finished he walked directly from the course and went back to his hotel. That week, his longest conversations were with his caddie, the mighty Jackie Leigh, because nobody else mattered that much or could contribute as much towards success.

Then it was the night before the championship and he

knew, also, what this feeling would be. No matter how much practice, no matter how well it had all gone, there was that dreadful panic that it had all been too late and not enough – that it would never be right in the morning.

His comfort was that he knew the others would be enduring the same doubts. It never varied. After his first round, when he trailed six strokes behind Lema, the leader, it might have seemed that his feeling of inadequacy was well-founded. And yet Thomson felt confident because he was convinced that none of them could keep up this pace and that, as the championship neared to its close, fear would take control of all of them.

In Lema's case, his scant preparation was perhaps the cause of that leading 68, since he had insufficient time to notice, and therefore worry about, the perils of Birkdale. But they would get to him before this week was out.

Thomson showed on the second day just how far he had removed himself from human contact when he emerged from the last green with a satisfying 68 which put him among the leaders. It is the custom, once the scorecard formalities have been completed, for the player to climb the rostrum in the Press tent and answer questions about his play.

This began as an American custom where journalists are reluctant to break sweat on a golf course but rather wait to be told – although in fairness it does mean that once the player has given his Press conference, he is left unmolested.

Some players use these conferences for impromptu cabaret, and men such as Doug Sanders, Sam Snead and Lee Trevino are welcome, no matter what their scores, simply for the entertainment they provide.

But Thomson was ill at ease with this elaborate ritual which had come into vogue since he had last won. It was new to him in Britain, and he refused to get on the stage, but instead remained in the doorway while the journalists clustered round him.

'You don't really want me in here do you?' he asked and

he could not resist during his brief discourse, a few sly digs at the writers, few of whom had seen him compile his score because he was not news. He was about to leave when he half-turned in the doorway and said: 'I'll come in and tell you all about it when it's over!' And we laughed. Only the winner comes in here when it is over and, in this sort of field, that had to be a Thomson joke.

I saw him standing alone behind the last green just after this episode and his manner was remote. On the other side of the fence stood a small boy,' autograph book poised. Thomson stood there for a few minutes gazing into the distance. I called his name and nodded towards the boy. Thomson woke up and signed. He had been so completely engrossed in his own thoughts, he had not noticed. He turned and walked away, not a word spoken.

The last day was a marathon 36 holes and he was two strokes behind the leaders at the start. His caddie Jackie had stationed friends and relatives round the course to work a bush-telegraph information network, so that Thomson would know at all times how the battle progressed. It was essential, because this could be a furious scrap with ten men covered by four strokes at the start of the day.

By lunchtime the lead had changed hands eleven times, but when the dust settled for the start of the last round, Thomson was clear. So far there had been no real crisis. But Thomson knew that he could not escape without one. It did not bother him overmuch, since, to him it was an attendant part of winning, and therefore could be expected and should not be feared.

He had long accepted the philosophy that winning was only part of what the man himself could do and mostly what others were doing. Thus it was pointless to worry about them overmuch, but essential to play each stroke as correctly as possible.

His problems began on the short twelfth, where he took three putts to complete the hole after a wayward tee shot. Then an indecisive tee shot on the thirteenth left him in long grass and his lead had diminished to one stroke with Lema, his close challenger and partner, just waiting for another error.

As they stepped to the fourteenth tee, Thomson knew that he had to stop this swing of fortune before it became irretrievable. He peered down this short hole towards the green and suddenly sensed that something was different about it. The wind had changed so imperceptibly that Lema had not noticed it, and Thomson had almost missed it. They were protected on the leeward side of a sandhill, but the flag in the distance was fluttering at a slightly different angle to the morning.

It needed more club, and Thomson drilled his ball into that distant green. Lema with only his notebook for an ally, had missed the green. This was the difference between Thomson's outlook and that of the new breed.

He had an instinct, a feel for the way a course should be played. His eyes, indeed all his senses, worked for him all the time he played his golf and he had no need of notebooks and yardage charts. And his ability to act on the evidence of his senses won him the British Open, since it halted any further advance by Lema, who wasted strokes on that hole.

The crisis had passed for Thomson, and his golf swing seemed unshackled as he played comfortably towards his fifth British Open. For others it had been a heartbreaking experience. In particular Brian Huggett could look back on four sixes in his scorecards and wonder what might have happened without them. As it was he finished joint second with Christy O'Connor, while Lema, not interested in anything but first place languished down the list.

Thomson bettered par over those finishing holes when his approach struck the seventeenth flagstick and earned him a gratuitous birdie. Then, with his drive safely launched down the last fairway towards the white clubhouse, he knew that it was over, and formally ended any doubt with a simple safe approach into the fat of the final green.

That year, it had been decided that the spectators should remain behind the chestnut fencing and thus avoid what the officials thought was the undignified scramble for a place around the last green.

It had always been more than just a wild stampede and somehow seemed to capture the unfettered jubilation of a winner who had kept himself and his nerve subdued for four rounds, and who at last could relax.

I walked alongside the then club secretary Colonel John Rees as Thomson marched towards that last green. The colonel looked up at the cheering crowds behind the fences and muttered: 'I said I'd keep them behind the railings and by God I did.'

At that moment I lost him in the crowd as the railings came down and the horde swarmed around Thomson. Nothing would ever break that tradition, and not when a man like Peter Thomson has come in from the cold.

Chapter 10: *Lee Trevino, Muirfield, 1972*

Trevino was a prisoner in the castle, trapped in the banqueting hall by a hundred people who drank mead and ate with their hands while minstrels serenaded them. He was trapped because he was their guest of honour, and it did not please him.

That afternoon he had arrived at Muirfield from the Canadian Open, which he had lost. Within two days he must defend his British Open title, and his first glance at Muirfield told him that he needed all the time that was left. He was tired and befuddled by the journey, and did not need a mock medieval banquet to waste the hours that should have been given to precious sleep.

Nicklaus and the rest of them had been at work for days on this course. Trevino had to believe that he could learn enough – if not as much – to start with a reasonable chance against them. But that meant total concentration on the task, and when his entourage had informed that he was due at this banquet in Dalhousie Castle, he refused to budge.

They had rented him a minor stately home called Yesterhouse for the week of the championship and he went to his room and shut the door. They had pleaded with him to change his mind. Not only would the guests be very disappointed if he failed to show, but also the headlines the next day would be damaging if the defending champion snubbed a dinner in his honour. Trevino grudgingly saw the sense of their arguments and agreed – but warned them never to spring this kind of duty on him again. He was there to play golf and that was all.

However, as that evening wore on, Trevino could not stay

angry, and gradually began to enjoy the party in his honour. He joined in the act himself when it was announced that the frail old man sitting next to him was the Mexican ambassador. The sight of him amused Trevino for he helped the old man to his feet and declared : Don't worry folks, it's the best we can do at the moment. But it'll get better !'

And then it was over, and Trevino knew that in the solitude of Yesterhouse he would sleep well that night. The next day he saw its spacious lawns and resolved that here he would prepare himself, away from the crowds, during this coming week.

The public expected too much of him; wanted him to turn the practice ground into a circus and to combine the antics of a clown with the artistry and skill of a high-wire act. There was a time when this was all he had to offer, but now he was champion, ranked alongside Nicklaus as the best exponent of golf in the world. Now he had to take himself seriously because he had a reputation to protect – that, now, was the main demand upon him.

He accepted, perhaps more than other professionals, that the practice ground routine was part of the show for the public, part of what they had paid to see, yet the style of practice he preferred offered very little spectator appeal.

The purpose of practice for him was to find, then tune, the tempo of this swing and to this end he was more interested in striking the ball than aiming for a target. He struck golf balls in practice at a faster rate than any other professional because this tempo had to be regained every day and, in his experience, once he had found the rhythm it was followed automatically by the accuracy.

Indeed there was a period in his early days when radio music was an essential part of his routine. It emphasised this rhythm quite apart from helping this gregarious personality to endure the loneliness of hours on the practice ground. He knew that his short, flat swing could not function adequately unless its tempo was correct, but most times he could not follow the rather unspectacular practice routine he desired. But this week, in the privacy of Yesterhouse, it would be possible.

Nicklaus had been hard at work for a week because he prepared himself in a different manner. He preferred to learn on the course and, in so doing, rehearse the kind of strokes required on each hole and in all conditions. And this time there was the additional incentive of his declared intention to land the Grand Slam of the four major titles in one season. Already he had the U.S. Masters and the U.S. Open to his credit and, as he had won at Muirfield in 1966 and had now put in more practice than anybody else, he was launched favourably on the British section of his Slam.

Nevertheless, Trevino did not feel grossly inadequate along-side such exhaustive preparations of the best golfer in the world. He knew that planning on these fickle seaside courses could be very dangerous. It was possible on American courses – tailored to a symmetrical fairness and with more predict-able weather conditions – to develop a repetitive knack which, with a sensible margin for error and fate, could be successful.

But this strategy could never be as reliable on a British links course, since each stroke on this rugged terrain pre-sented a fresh test, different in its demands from any pre-viously played. Even if a drive landed within a yard of an earlier spot, such were the humps and hollows that the sub-sequent stroke could be a new experience, no matter how much practice had gone before.

It was difficult, therefore, to measure the real value of Nicklaus's protracted practice since, given a working know-ledge, a surfeit of preparation could be damaging and pro-duce a fixed strategy. More than this, it could develop within the player too much respect for the course, and provoke an inhibiting awareness of its problems and difficulties.

In any case, it should not take a professional at the height of his prowess more than two rounds to assess a golf course, sort out his amoury and adjust it to the particular demands. Trevino's punching type of swing made transition to the smaller British golf ball less traumatic, and if he was short on his homework, then at least it gave him a healthy disrespect for Muirfield.

Even before that championship began, Nicklaus was falling victim of his own preparation, seeing more of the perils of Muirfield each day and realising the damage they could cause. Quite early in his practice week, he knew the course as well as he needed, yet he forced himself to discover all its moods, in every kind of wind. Sometimes he would wait in the Greywalls Hotel alongside the course for the wind to change, so that he could learn more about the course.

This diligence had another destroying effect because when he came to the championship he was horrified to see that the wind was now coming from yet another direction – and one that he had not experienced during his week's work. It was, in fact, a different golf course – as new in playing characteristics to Nicklaus as it was to Trevino. The notes on club selection, the landmarks from which he measured his distances to the green, now had to be revised, and he had to do his learning during the championship itself.

He was plagued by his cowering respect for Muirfield and his ignorance of its new mood. For three days he trooped meekly around the course. Then on the last day, when he had run out of time, he realised that Muirfield should not be that punitive to a man of his class, and he cut loose with a 66, having declared the night before that he would do something in the low sixties.

That declaration proved that he could have produced that kind of golf much earlier – if not in the first round then probably in the second and most certainly in the third, when he really needed it to give himself room to manoeuvre over the last day.

That will be his lasting frustrating memory of failure at

Muirfield where he missed the title – and further interest in the Grand Slam – by a stroke. The ability was there all the time, but he could not, or would not stir it into action. Perhaps he was powerless to do so until circumstances offered no other course.

Had Nicklaus put too much pressure on himself by declaring openly that the Grand Slam was possible? Only a man of his capabilities could dare to consider it. He possessed a range of shots beyond all others, and championships seemed to inspire rather than inhibit him.

In the third round when Nicklaus was still jogging gently along, assuming that Muirfield would catch the others, Trevino cut loose and forced himself to the front – so, for the third year in succession, he went into the last round of the British Open as leader. In the process, Trevino almost hammered Jacklin's hope out of shape, but even at this early stage – with Nicklaus slumbering to his own doom – these two men resolved that the championship rested between them. They knew clearly of Nicklaus's talent, but the absence of any sign that it was beginning to erupt gave them cause for hope and, as they moved deeper into the championship, they knew that he was leaving it too late.

By the sixteenth tee of that third round, Jacklin and Trevino, paired together, were level at the front of the field and both hit nondescript tee shots to this short hole and found bunkers.

Trevino's plight was even worse than Jacklin's. His ball was stuck in a greenside bunker, on the downslope of fine sand. There was precious little working space between himself and the flagstick, and he would have to dig deep with his wedge to give the ball the halting spin it required to save his par-three.

He reached for his Helen Hicks wedge, a ladies club with a knife-edged blade which he had brought over specially because it could cut through fine sand more effectively. He stood in the bunker, his stocky frame twisting from side to side to screw his spikes into the sand for firm anchorage.

His white baseball cap was pulled down so tightly over his eyes that it seemed to obscure his vision as he looked at the flagstick a couple of times, the club gently wavering in his hand as if he were trying to guess its weight. Then he began to move. The club eased back then down towards the ball. The spectators waited for the spray of sand and the ball that would rise through it.

But something went wrong. He dipped awkwardly at the moment of contact and the ball took off like a bullet. In that split second every witness, Trevino included, saw disaster – this awful stroke had thinned the ball so strongly that it could not possibly remain on the green. Its flight was lost as the heads turned to await its arrival on the other side of the green. But it never arrived. There was a crack and by the time the heads turned back, the ball had disappeared down the hole.

Trevino's frightful stroke had hit the flagstick at such a precise point that it had run down the stick and into the hole for a birdie two. As that ball left him Trevino was convinced that, at best, he would take five and that would certainly give Jacklin the lead (and the Englishman always wins the big ones from in front).

As that ball dropped into the hole, Trevino was already leading. Jacklin, from another bunker at the back of the green, had no possible hopes of matching that birdie – certainly not after that dramatic episode. So Jacklin fell behind. But even then Trevino had not quite finished with him.

As they reached the last green Jacklin, on the front of the green, suggested that Trevino should play his chip shot from the back of the green first. It occurred to Jacklin that this was the kind of stroke that the American could hole – and he was perfectly correct. Trevino tickled the ball directly into the hole.

On the final day they were paired together again, and though Trevino, after his experience at Birkdale the previous year, was prepared for any partisanship in the crowd, he suspected it would be minimal.

This was a largely Scottish gallery and Jacklin was not quite so much the man of the people here. The Scots wanted good golf, a good contest and a worthy champion, and Nicklaus, Trevino or Jacklin would fulfil all these qualifications simply from the way the championship was perched at that stage.

Through that long afternoon both men played each other, yet could not forget Nicklaus because the scoreboards told them that he was consuming the course. Yet he was not taking large enough bites, and his earlier caution and confusion hung now like a millstone around his neck. He knew he needed a low score and that meant taking all the risks at a time when any errors would be irredeemable and the men leading him were playing with discretion. And no matter how great his competitive powers, it was doubtful that he could forget that the Grand Slam hung on this, his last round.

So, they resolved, it was between the two of them, and they had long been acquaintances. Both relied heavily on inspiration, so that each knew the dangers of the other while there was even an inch of the course still remaining. Both had fluctuating temperaments, although Trevino's was more apparent through his banter, and Jacklin, though equally sensitive, did not have Trevino's quick powers of recovery.

Even so the odds might have favoured Jacklin in that last round but for a near-phobia that was building within him about Trevino, and in particular, the American's perpetual chatter.

It irritated Jacklin, but his mistake was to let it be known that it bothered him. Yet not once during the closing holes did Trevino give any evidence that he had capitalised on Jacklin's irritation. In any case, Jacklin, with two world championships to his credit, could have been expected to have acquired a more protective shell against these outside influences.

By the time they reached the long seventeenth hole they were level, and both knew now that one error, or one superior stroke, could resolve this championship. Trevino had to play first and stood up to the ball and was about to swing. But on the last forward glance before he cranked his swing into life, he saw a T.V. crewman in his line of fire and stepped away. In that moment, the spell was broken, the cocoon that kept him removed from the world had been shattered.

It was as though Trevino had been stabbed and the adrenalin was gushing out. He had lost step with the drama, missed his precise cue in time when the ball should have been fired and probably fired perfectly. The flow and sequence had been disrupted and when he stepped back to the ball, he was like a man trying to remember what should have been, but knowing it had eluded him.

He swung, and the ball took off towards a bunker down the fairway, disappearing into its depths. Before he reached there, Trevino knew he could not force a scoring stroke from that pit and that nothing, save an inadequate lob back to the fairway would be possible.

In that moment Trevino believed he had given the Open to Jacklin, and the feeling was mutual because in that bunker far ahead was the proof that Jacklin needed that this championship had been marked down for him, and that he would now demonstrate that the first Open he had won had not been solely a glorious stroke of fortune. The public always demanded constant proof of class, and here it was.

He jumped at the ball and lashed it hard into perfect position far down the fairway. Now he was safe, because he sensed that Trevino would have to struggle every inch to the green and that he himself must emerge from the hole with at least a one-stroke advantage. The weight of pressure was already beginning to lift from Jacklin; he experienced an uplifting excitement, a tightening knot of joy in his stomach, as he realised that it was nearly over and that he would be champion.

Trevino tamely rescued his ball from the sand and deposited it a few unhelpful yards up the fairway. He was still behind Jacklin's magnificent drive and therefore had to play his third stroke. The best he could now hope for was to find the green with his three-wood, but even he sensed that it was already over, and his aim with that club showed that he had lost interest.

The ball fizzed left and he waited for it to drift back into the centre, but it remained on its disaster course and vanished into the long grass short of the green as if to remind Trevino that there was little point in going on with this charade.

Trevino watched sadly as Jacklin settled over his second stroke which would inevitably put the ball on the green. Here endeth the contest, the preparation, the effort, the turmoil. What, short of disaster, was left? There had been enough trouble on this hole already and it had only a certain amount to offer.

Jacklin, borne on by the crowds, by Trevino's mistake and by the close proximity of his second title, could not fail now, and as he let fly the ball sprang into life. A faint hope flickered in Trevino's breast as he realised that this ball, too, was going left away from the green. But although it landed in the area where Trevino's ball languished, it toppled down to give Jacklin an even stance.

Nothing had really changed except that Jacklin was irritated by this small error because it meant that he had to work a little harder than he had planned. Trevino took very little time over his recovery from the rough, and it seemed that he wanted this miserable affair to end quickly.

He jabbed harshly at the ball, with scant intent or judgement, and it cleared the rough, ignored the green and finished on the back fringe. He had now taken four strokes and each of them had conspired to hand this title to Jacklin within the next ten minutes.

Jacklin settled briskly over his chip shot and as he made contact with the ball, the faint tremor running through his hands and arms told him it had been struck as he wished. His head still down, he assessed that the ball would finish close and that the crowd would roar approval before he needed to look.

The cheering began, but never reached its crescendo. Instead, it tailed off into a moan, and when Jacklin looked up the ball was only halfway to the hole. The stroke had been pathetic. He was surprised but not yet worried, even though he was making unnecessarily hard work of winning this title.

He walked forward, marked his ball and waited impatiently for Trevino to play. The crowd, too, was a little restless, as if wanting this supporting act to get out of the way so that the star could command the stage. Part of their mood hung on the fact that Jacklin's ball was not close enough and the championship had not fully taken definite shape. Trevino must take two more to get down. If Jacklin holed his own putt, he held a two stroke lead going into the last. If he missed, then it was one stroke and still enough, but only just.

Trevino stepped up to his chip shot and without purpose touched the ball downhill towards the hole. It had been played well enough, the way Trevino always plays these little ones, and its pace was good as it homed on the hole. Then it dropped.

By some instinctive act of skill and unwitting judgement, Trevino's chip shot which began as an act of unconditional surrender had fallen into the hole. His mind was elsewhere when he struck that ball, yet the body, drilled by a lifetime of self discipline, took command and produced the perfect stroke. It had been perfectly played if imperfectly conceived.

Jacklin saw it and at first could not comprehend it. The hysterical, overwhelming roar of the crowd added to his feeling of helplessness, and he felt like a condemned man who realises in that last split second that the trapdoor has opened and he is falling. He tried to stand back from the situation, but could not.

He had this next putt for the lead. That was all he had to remember, and yet somehow the mathematics were no longer important or, rather, Trevino's outrageous stroke had dwarfed them. Jacklin stood over a putt that would give him the lead in the British Open – and most assuredly the title – yet everybody sensed that he was fighting for his life.

He crouched low and was locked there as if fighting his inner thoughts. The pressure was tearing him apart and shaking the very last drops of will power from him. The putt was awful, a muscle spasm which sent the ball too strong and too wide.

Trevino was astounded when he saw the length of Jacklin's return putt and realised that this championship was not yet over. It was three feet and at the end of the day, and in this hysterical moment, it took on stifling proportions. The door had been closed on Trevino but Jacklin had forgotten to bolt it.

As Jacklin stood over the return putt, it was already a lost cause. He stood there lifelessly, as though forgetting what he was supposed to do. He had already lost and now the ritual had to catch up with the reality. He had had this Open sewn up until a few minutes ago and now, as he missed the return, he was like a punch-drunk boxer no longer in control but enduring by instinct even though it was futile.

Trevino was now one stroke clear, and he allowed Jacklin to walk ahead of him to the last tee so that this incredible turn of events could sink in on the Englishman. In fact he had no need of such strategy because Jacklin was already finished, lost in his own bewildered world, not sure why it had happened.

The American had another reason for taking his time to reach that last tee. The last few minutes had been difficult for him to comprehend, and he wanted no time now to dwell on them, nor to contemplate the terrors of the last hole.

He wanted to tee the ball, glance once down the fairway and swing. This he did, with Jacklin now looking like a shell-shock victim. There was nothing left for him to give, and he stumbled down that last fairway losing touch, and able to finish only in third place behind Nicklaus.

The episode will be remembered firstly because it was the Open that Jacklin threw away, but perhaps more importantly because it showed that, no matter how constantly the world's greatest golfers drill themselves to near perfection, the pressure of situations can force them into simple and stupid errors. Therein lies the truth, if ever doubted, that the game is greater than the man.

Chapter 11: *The Walker Cup, St. Andrews, 1971*

Bonallack had asked them not to read newspapers until the match was over since whatever was written about them could be only disturbing, whether good or bad. There had been too much work, too much effort aimed at building this team's morale to ruin it all now by the written word which, anyway, would tell them what they already knew – the record book showed they had no chance of winning the Walker Cup.

Most of the young fellows in his team would heed his instruction, and not have papers delivered to their rooms in the morning, and if the older ones ignored it, then at least they were experienced enough to cope with newspaper opinions.

But this was not his main preoccupation as he sat alone in his suite at the Old Course Hotel alongside the seventeenth hole. The newspaper edict was a minor precaution, perhaps no more than just another sign to his team as to how seriously he regarded this match with the Americans, and how much he wanted to win it. Now he must arrange his team in its most effective fighting order, and what he needed most of all was a good start from the first morning's foursomes. If it was too hopeful to expect a lead, then at least his men should trail by no more than a point as they went into the afternoon singles.

This was a young American side that had come to St Andrews, and Bonallack suspected that they had not given themselves enough time to learn the course, nor were they getting the correct kind of advice from the more experienced men in the side on how to play the Old Course.

The British had been hard at work months before this match – in the early stages on their home courses – perfecting, or at least improving, the pitch-and-run stroke which Bonallack had insisted would be of paramount importance on this course.

Then Bonallack had brought them all to St Andrews for a rehearsal a month before the match, and his task had been simply to dispel the myth that St Andrews was a formidable and unfair test. And yet this exercise, too, had benefits beyond the short term, since it served to build upon the sense of belonging, the team spirit, which he wanted among his men.

If the Americans thought that St Andrews was eccentric then this, too, suited his purpose, since it would fill them with negative thoughts about their own chances. Yet now, as Bonallack sat alone, he wondered whether he had worked hard enough on his men, and whether all the effort of morale-boosting had given them enough protection to permit their talents to function under the pressures to come.

He had thought that the younger ones would have needed more encouragement, but was surprised to discover that they exuded a massive confidence and were fearlessly anxious to get into the fight. For them, there were no bad memories of previous defeats, and they simply wanted the chance to assert themselves against whatever was presented. But Bonallack's memories stretched back over many defeats, and some of them of the worst kind – when the British team should have won but stumbled in the act.

Now, the winning of the Walker Cup had become something of an obsession in his life, since he could no longer contrive the kind of enthusiasm that had spurred him to so many personal triumphs. As his string of personal championships grew longer, the compulsion to win became proportionately weaker.

But the Walker Cup remained. It was elusive and yet the frustration of it all was that he knew some British teams had been good enough to win it, and that one victory since this international series had started was not a real reflection of the differing standards between American and British golf.

There had been Baltimore in 1965, with Townsend, Clark and Shade in the side, and that first day when they had returned to their downtown hotel with an 8–3 lead, deliriously happy since they could not see this dispirited and ragged American side shaking itself from its depression. And even by lunchtime on that final day, when the British needed only two points from the singles matches, the only doubt had been which two men would earn those points first to capture the trophy for Britain.

What an awful presumption that had been when the Americans counter-attacked viciously and the British, each thinking that the others would save him, fell like ninepins, and only Gordon Cosh, the Scot, delivered his skipper Joe Carr a point.

Then only Clive Clark's match against John Hopkins remained alive – and even he was one down with two holes to play. By all that was just, Clark should have squared that match on the short seventeenth hole up the hill. Hopkins shanked his tee shot into the depths of the pine forest, and not only should Hopkins never have found the ball but also, if discovered, it should have been unplayable.

But Hopkins found it, played it, and halved the hole. And only a putt which tram-lined a path across the last green gave Clark a birdie three which halved his personal match and tied the series with the United States. There had been no glory for any of them there save Clark, who had withstood admirably the pressures of responsibility to save his team the hideous embarrassment of defeat.

Two years later, when they met the Americans at Royal St Georges in Sandwich, there had been no such surprise in defeat because the best of the British had gone, and the Americans arrived with a team which included, Murphy (a

top money winner on the American circuit within a year);
Fleckman (who led the U.S. Open for three rounds) together with Dickson, Cerrudo, Grant and Lewis, all of whom
turned professional and became substantial money earners,
and winners.

Milwaukee in 1969 had been close, and if Critchley and
Craddock had held their leads instead of slipping to halved
matches, the trophy might have come back to Britain. But
then everybody shared in that defeat, and the frustration of
it had been that they were so close to victory.

Bonallack felt confident about the men he had brought
this time to St Andrews. They were keyed-up and anxious to
play. Their last-minute problems were handled by the wise
tutor John Jacobs, who knew that it was not golf instruction
but simply reassurance that these young men needed at this
moment before the conflict began.

They knew the course well enough, not only from the practice, but also from the lengthy team talks in Bonallack's
room, when each hole had been analysed and they had
talked about strategy. They had talked about the value of
the pitch-and-run stroke, and while all of it was intrinsically
useful, the overall effect was to build even more on this feeling of team spirit and the boosting thought that they were
better prepared to cope with the Old Course than the
Americans.

His men had done their part in the preparations, and now
he must do his in formulating them into an effective force.
He had been helped in his task by the wisdom and
experience of the teams's chief selector, Sandy Sinclair – a
Scot with an instinctively correct judgement of a golfer,
which had served him so well during his own playing
days.

How should they be blended? It was pointless to send out
the youngsters, Roddy Carr and Warren Humphreys, together, because the strain would be too much – or would
it? They might form a fearless and winning combination.

But it was too early to take chances. Bonallack needed as close as he could get to a *guarantee* of a good start.

So both young men had to be paired with experienced players. He put Carr with big Charlie Green, the genial Scot, since both were long hitters and slightly erratic, and neither would be alarmed by wildness in the other, nor would either find himself in odd regions of the course to which he was unaccustomed.

David Marsh, the Southport general practitioner, had an admirable bedside manner, and this patience and understanding could disarm the most tense person. And while the Scot, George McGregor, was not burningly intense, his relentless steadiness could at least be matched by Marsh and make them an efficient partnership.

Scott MacDonald, a man of greater intensity, possessed an urgency to win that sometimes expected too much from his partners, so the unflappable Yorkshireman Rodney Foster was the ideal companion. Rodney's temper never faltered even in the most extreme circumstances, and it was impossible ever to tell from his countenance whether he had just gained a crushing victory or suffered a horrible defeat. For all this, his golf possessed an incisive quality made all the more lethal because it took so many otherwise enchanted opponents by surprise.

That left four of them to place, but two would have to sit out, and Bonallack felt that Marks and Stuart, both better individualists, would be needed for that ability in the afternoon singles. So he decided to pair himself with young Humphreys, with whom he had played effectively in England team matches.

He had made his choice, and only the next day's events would tell whether it had been the right one. By lunchtime he had his answer, and the Americans had been crushed 4–0 in the opening foursomes matches. There had never been such a glorious British offensive on the first day, and it was the Americans who nosed out timidly like frightened rabbits.

It seemed too good to be true, and away beyond anything Bonallack believed possible. It seemed inconceivable that the Americans would remain downtrodden, or as oppressed as they had been in this opening bout, for the rest of the match. He was correct, because not only did the Americans struggle back into the fight by the afternoon singles, but also, at the end of the day, they were leading. Bonallack was angry at the British capitulation to which he had contributed. Four matches had slipped to the Americans on the last hole.

It served to convince him that the two teams were evenly matched, and that therefore his team could win, provided that he correctly disposed the British force over the last day.

None of his team had played badly, but this faltering finish had undermined their efforts. There were no excuses, although he himself could have been forgiven for the loss of his own point to Vinny Giles, a young man of impudent talent.

They had been level as they came to the seventeenth, and the American, torn mentally between the perils at the front of the green and the penalties of the road behind it, let fly too strongly with his approach and the ball trickled off the green and on to the road.

Bonallack had sensibly struck his ball to the safe part of the green, and was some six feet from the hole. He waited with gathering confidence as Giles fussed over his stroke from the road, because it was obvious that the American would have to scramble as best he could to save this hole.

Giles jabbed the ball up the bank, and it ran down into the hole leaving a dumbfounded Bonallack still outraged at such daylight robbery, even when they had finished their match – and Giles had taken the point without a word of apology.

There had been no serious flaw in the playing ability of Bonallack's team, but their weakness was simply a lack of mental stamina to stay in the fight until it was really over.

More than this, that weakness which brought about the American revival was now a bad and vivid memory to all of them, and was itself a difficulty which had to be overcome.

His team's morale had been shaken severely, and his task now was to shake them out of the fatalistic mood which might descend upon them. All the time-worn clichés would not help him now, since his men had tasted the battle and knew for themselves the reality of it all.

Bonallack had to find a way of making them forget what had happened, or at least contrive a situation which would make them concentrate more fully on the present. And suddenly it came to him. He would force them to think of this as a fresh start, as a new challenge, by giving them little chance of coincidence with the previous day.

He would mix up his superbly successful foursomes pairings of the previous day, because to send out the old pairings would serve only to remind them of how it had all turned sour on them. But a new partner would engross them and perhaps restore the edge to their golf. It was a risk, but it was better than repetition.

He wrote down the names of Charlie Green and Geoff Marks. Both were big hitters and got on well together. Carr was paired with Hugh Stuart. Bonallack placed himself with Marsh. McDonald? He was best left with Foster. Humphreys would be rested because he was needed for the singles in the afternoon which, even if the morning went well, must become a desperately close fight.

Bonallack consulted Sandy Sinclair, who accepted that such a drastic shake-up might just come off and at least was worth the attempt. Others would criticise Bonallack without knowing the reason, and because it was only a partial success and not as good as Bonallack had intended.

The changes certainly gave the players more to think about and no time to worry about the previous day. But they were still unsettled and did not really get into their stride, so that by lunchtime on that final day, the Americans were two points clear.

Yet Bonallack was still confident, and believed that the American lead did not give a true account of the strength of that side. They were losing confidence and if his own men could maintain a constant pressure on them during the singles, he was convinced the Americans would buckle.

There were other reasons, unknown to Bonallack, for the increasing improvement in the British chance. The American side lacked cohesion and perhaps an adequate depth of team spirit. In times past it had been possible to cull young men from all parts of the United States, some of them strangers, fit them out in blazers, and call them a team. Certainly, when the British opposition had been weak, the individual talents of these men, playing for themselves, had been enough to prevail.

But the gathering crisis of St Andrews would demand more than that; a responsibility that should have forced more from each man. Bonallack had worked assiduously to put his own men in this mood, but his counterpart, John Winters, had thought, as other American captains, that the selection of the ten best American amateur golfers was enough in itself.

There had been little attempt at developing team spirit, and indeed though two older experienced men – Bill Hyndman and Bill Campbell – had been placed in this young side to give it a working knowledge of the Old Course, this aspect was never fully discussed at their team meetings. They had not been told just how important the pitch-and-run stroke could be on the Old Course, and Bonallack had seen for himself when McDonald and Foster forced a half point in the morning foursomes, how the Americans relied heavily on their wedge-play in a crisis. That, he was convinced, would ruin them, if only his men could keep close and force the errors.

So the afternoon began, and for the spectators there seemed no cause for hope. Most felt that the Americans would find their pace and then move clear, and for a long time as the two sides remained deadlocked, they wondered just how long the British could hold on. Then, suddenly, something about the British resistance and its duration gave a glimmer of hope. Now, it seemed that the teams really were finely balanced, and that one slight shift in the pattern would send the match falling into one camp or the other.

It is a curious aspect of team golf that, while for each player it remains an individual demand, it can be greatly affected by outside influences of the rest of the team. Winning and losing in this atmosphere is a highly contagious disease, and it needs news of only one man's success to filter back through to his team-mates for them to gather strength from it.

Bonallack was to explain afterwards: 'When you find the fellow in front of you is winning and so is the chap in front of him, there is a great feeling of elation, and that confidence spreads into your own golf.'

The winning of the Walker Cup took just an hour, and it was around four o'clock in the afternoon, with the sky showing traces of the gathering dusk, that the explosive cheering began. It came from one part of the course, and then another, and each time as it changed direction, its intensity told that it could signal only a rise in British fortunes.

It was difficult for Bonallack, engaged in a losing struggle with Lanny Wadkins, to know exactly what great deeds were going on around him, but he could tell from the cheering that his men were prevailing, and each American player sensed this change. The sheer partisan delight of that crowd began to take its own toll on American morale and, when Humphreys and Stuart won their matches to bring the series level, Bonallack knew that it now hung on finishing power – the quality his men had lacked on the previous day.

At least Bonallack was thankful that he had placed his anchor man David Marsh in the seventh position and not at the bottom of the list. From past experience he knew that, in a tight match, it could all be over before the eighth man had the chance to prove his effectiveness. It was more important for the middle of his batting order to mop up what points were available, and Marsh would be there to maintain that offensive if he was needed.

The pendulum had now swung towards the British, and the news spread around the town, whispered in shops, passed on by strangers in the street, so that it seemed the entire population had flocked to the course to witness this small piece of history.

The American spirit had withered, and each man dismally seemed to accept the prospect of defeat, yet carried on as if by reflex to the last green. Match after match arrived there, and the American, falling back on the instinct of a lifetime, reached for a wedge to guide the ball safely over the Valley of Sin. It was the wrong stroke, since it gave the ball height but little power and left the Americans too far from the flagstick for a reasonable chance of holing the putt.

Miller, Simons and Gabrielsen went like lemmings to their doom by this process, then Hyndman, his ageing nerve already shattered by a master stroke from Marsh into the previous green, gave up the ghost and the Walker Cup on the last green.

It was over – and Bonallack laid hands on the Walker Cup. Amid the wild celebrations that followed that evening in the Old Course Hotel, Bonallack nevertheless felt a sense of loss, and did not know the reason. It was only months later that he realised that the driving force had gone. He had won countless championships and could not be obsessed by them any more. The American Amateur had never been more than a gratuitous thought, and it had not bothered him that he had never won. But the Walker Cup had seemed unreachable. That had been his compulsion, and now it was done. To do it again would not be the same. Nothing, for Bonallack, would ever be the same again.

Chapter 12: *Ken Venturi,*
Congressional, Washington, 1964

The door of the church was locked, but Venturi could see a light somewhere and knew that if he knocked long and loud enough somebody would let him in. He needed to pray, but not only that. He also needed to be alone.

This was the end of his road, and there could be no more chances after this week. His reputation lay in tatters, and he had been dismissed and forgotten. His self-esteem had diminished and all but disappeared, so that, if he persisted in the face of the failure of this week, it would be the worst kind of self-delusion.

Yet, he could not bring himself to prepare for the possibility that his great talent had suddenly fizzled out, and that he was now as helpless as if he had been struck blind. When he thought about all that he had achieved it seemed incredible that a talent could vanish without trace. It was more, now, than just the golf, because that was no longer the real crisis in his life. Around some corner, half-hidden, was the horrifying possibility that his life, as he had chosen to pursue it, had been wasted.

He knelt, gazing at the darkened altar, needing to believe that the spiritual pain and anguish of the last few years had not gone unnoticed by his Maker, yet knowing that it was a monstrous presumption to assume that God himself might be moved by the profound reversal in Venturi's life.

What else was there? It was the presumption of a simple faith that demanded that, if nothing else, somebody was watching it all and was mutely sympathetic. If it was too much to be delivered from this anguish then at least he could plead for the spiritual strength to endure it.

He also knew that he was asking for much more. He wanted to win again because that was the only justification he had ever known in life. He was still enough of a professional to trust his own judgement, and he knew that his swing, even though changed, was good enough to work.

But he had lost confidence with himself, and could not trust himself in moments of crisis. This pernicious disease had shown itself first on a golf course, and then gradually spread through his life. At first it had been the fear of a particularly difficult stroke when no other would do.

No matter how often he tried to convince himself that he had the skill to execute the stroke, he backed away from it. There had been a time when he relished the difficult moments since they gave him the chance to demonstrate his talent, but now those same crises were met with unconditional surrender.

He had covered the ground about where and why it had all gone wrong so many times. He was a proud young man, and maybe the greater the pride the greater the fall. But there had been a time when he possessed an arrogance which convinced him that he was better than all of them. He had even convinced himself that he had outgrown his mentor Byron Nelson, and that he had nothing more to teach him. His horizon was limitless and even the newspapers, with one accord, promised that he would be greater than Hogan, Snead, Jones and the rest.

He had almost won the U.S. Masters as an amateur and remained certain that he would have done so, had not the Augusta officials broken with tradition which allowed the last day leader to play with Byron Nelson. It was felt that these two men were too close, and so Venturi was paired with another player and shot an 80 – to lose the title by one stroke.

The transfer to professionalism had only underlined the

potential of his talent, and in four years he was earning a lot of money, collecting tournament wins and being heralded as the next great man in golf.

Perhaps it was Palmer who started the decline, not directly, but with his booming power golf. In 1960, Augusta officials were scouring the locker-rooms for a Venturi-size green jacket when Palmer birdied himself into the title over the closing holes. This man laced the ball hard and it worked, and while Nelson and the others affirmed that Palmer could not endure with that kind of swing, Venturi could see that Palmer's style brought results, while he himself had yet to win a major title.

Thus he resolved to find more power, and to ignore the advice that his orthodox swing would go on for ever and must be rewarded soon. He had faded the ball with a left-to-right trajectory all his life because this was the safe way to play golf. Now he decided to learn how to hook for extra distance.

Venturi went to work, against the advice of his friends and even Ed Lowery, the man who had guided him throughout his golf career from those childhood days. Lowery had done all that he could for Venturi, offering him a business as an amateur so that he could play more competitive golf without financial worries (although Venturi turned it down to turn professional).

But now even Lowery despaired of him, and said: 'Kenny, have you got a dictionary in your house? Go home and look up the world HUMBLE. You have no idea of the meaning of the word.'

After that, but not because of it, Venturi's career turned sour. The winning stopped as he tried to accomplish it with a new kind of golf swing. Then he had been afflicted by mysterious pains in his chest and arms, and the doctors, while treating him, advised him to rest from tournament golf.

He was a worried man because he was no longer successful, and in his panic he ignored the doctors and forced himself through the pain to practise harder. But the pain was changing his swing and as he sought instinctively to avoid the sharp spasms, his technique underwent a change of its own. He found a way to get the swing over quickly.

Then the pain passed, but the quick flat golf swing remained and plunged him deeper into failure and, with it, despair. If he could have found merciful obscurity it might have helped, but his prestige – and maybe the desire for revenge by those he had slighted in the good days – kept his purgatory very public.

He slipped even further until nobody wanted him. The big tournaments could do without him and sometimes a small event would take him only because there was a familiar ring to the name. No matter how hard he pushed himself on the practice ground, the old confidence would not return and he began to stammer, his face twitched and he even tried medical treatment, but without success.

Then the money began to run out. He was almost broke, and was forced to borrow money to see him through another season. But even with the money to play, he still had to beg his way into some of the major tournaments, as he could not qualify on his record. He reached his lowest depth, when he realised that Augusta was not going to invite him to play in the Masters – and he had almost won it twice!

It was then that Venturi realised that, unless he came to trust his technique and himself, he might as well quit tournament golf, because he was wasting too much time and causing his family too much unnecessary grief. Better to be a club pro somewhere than have his family hovering on the breadline because of some futile conviction that remained within him.

He faced the first real test in the Thunderbird Classic of 1964, when he reached a point that called for the perfect stroke. If he retreated now, and took the easy way out, he was finished and would have no excuse for those few – even Lowery – who had kept faith with him all through this

Dr David Marsh walks across the eighteenth green to be congratulated by American Bill Hyndman on the 1971 British victory in the Walker Cup.

Left: Venturi, after his 12 ft. birdie putt at the ninth, during the final round of the 1964 U.S. Open.

Right: Portrush, 1951; a smiling Max Faulkner receives the Championship trophy from Brig. Noel Martin, the Royal Portrush Captain.

WORLD MATCH
PLAY FINAL, 1967.
Right: The
Champion, Arnold
Palmer, jubilant
after holing a long
putt which put him
one up in the match.

Left: Australian
Peter Thomson
watches, one-
legged, his putt
on the eighteenth
green.

Nicklaus and Jacklin shake hands at the end of the 1969
Ryder Cup.

OLYMPIC, 1966. *Above:* Intense delight of Bill Casper at dropping a 25 ft. putt for a birdie three on the eleventh hole. *Below* Left: Casper takes the lead in play-off game with (*Below Right*) Arnold Palmer, who tries to wave in the ball but fails.

Dai Rees, 'chaired', with the Ryder Cup.

St Andrews 1964. Lema the uninhibited – despite a lack of
knowledge of the course.

Above: Lema thanks his caddie, Tip Anderson, after winning the British Open in 1964.

Left: Gary Player, 1968 British Open Champion, with the trophy.

trouble. He struck the ball perfectly. He relied on Ken Venturi for the first time in many years, and he earned a big cheque.

Now, as he knelt in that church before the start of the U.S. Open at the Congressional course in Washington, he knew that what he needed was the assurance that the spark of self-reliance that had shown itself in the Thunderbird Classic would stay with him – even if it never burned again with the great intensity once had. Even if he failed this week, that would be enough to make the rest of his life bearable, particularly when he would consider what was and what might have been.

He left the church and for the next two days remained hidden among the pack of challengers for the U.S. Open, taking professional satisfaction from the efficiency of his golf swing, which worked with comfort.

He had been helped greatly by a letter from Father Kevin Murray, a San Francisco priest, who had counselled Venturi through all his troubles and wrote now saying that the pain and the suffering and the turmoil had all been essential ingredients for the formation of his new character, and that there was a strength of spirit within him now that would not yield.

On the third day, Venturi almost tore the course apart in the morning when he attacked with the lethal savagery of the old days. He ignored the stifling heat, and that morning had been so anxious to play that he had dispensed with a full breakfast. It was a silly mistake because he suffered acute heat prostration over the closing holes, and began to make silly strokes as his hands trembled. Mercifully the round finished before he could do his scorecard too much damage, and he was two strokes behind the leader with one round to play that afternoon.

But Venturi had done serious damage to himself, and a doctor advised him to lie down in the locker-room during the lunch break and to combat the heat exhaustion with some salt tablets washed down with iced tea. The Pressmen, sensing a story, were told there was a grave possibility that Venturi would have to quit. But then came the message: 'Venturi says he will be on the first tee for the final round, and would rather die than quit.'

It was a nice quote, and it also happened to be true, because Venturi was not going to back off from this one, even when his mind and body screamed for him to quit.

There had been too much pain, too many other moments when it had been easier to back off, and now he was too close to the prize to give up. But this was not just for the prize, although that did matter. This was a duel between Venturi and himself, and he had retreated too often in the past.

But now he was a different man. He must be, otherwise all the punishing hours he had toiled to rebuild his golf swing had been wasted. Was Father Murray right? Was there really a new Venturi? Or was the old one fooling himself?

The next three hours would divulge the answer, and Venturi knew he could not avoid them even if, in the extreme, it cost him his life. He was to lose contact with his surroundings as he played that last round, and was not even aware that officials had asked a doctor to stay by his side.

He was semi-conscious through the heat and the pain, and he moved like a sleep-walker, aware only of the ball and the changing fairway or flagstick to which it had to be struck. Somebody, perhaps the doctor, draped a cold towel over his head to forestall, perhaps for only a few more minutes, the moment when Venturi would fall down with heat exhaustion. He had no idea how the others had fared, but suddenly, even though he was not aware of it, the only threat to Venturi was himself and his weakening condition. Venturi had only to stay on his feet to win, but even that seemed an insuperable task.

However, this comatose state into which he was sinking had the great benefit of dulling his nerves and fears, so that his golf swing could work by instinct. Through the mists of semi-consciousness, he could see the last fairway. The cheering around him was a thousand miles away, and somebody told him he was four strokes clear as his legs fought the last few yards to the green. He dragged them painfully, his head bowed so that he could see the ground and realise that he was still moving.

Then the putter was in his hands. Then the ball. The stroke and somebody said : 'Hold your head up Ken. You're champion now.' And somehow that wasn't quite so important for Venturi in that moment.

Chapter 13: *Max Faulkner, Portrush, 1951*

Faulkner reached out in the darkness and switched on his bedside lamp, then he looked at his watch and realised that he had been awake for hours. It was impossible to sleep. He had told himself a thousand times that this unwanted vigil served no purpose and what tomorrow would bring was inevitable, and that there would be no answers to his questions until the end of the day.

But none of this logic calmed his tightening nerves, nor dulled his brain, nor relaxed his muscles. He was disturbed by the presence of tomorrow like a man who wakes, anxiously alert, in the dark, sensing that there is somebody or something close to him.

He was imprisoned in a dark silence, the minutes dragged slowly, and he wondered in that hushed hotel whether anybody was awake save himself. But then nobody else had reason to be awake, since he was the man with the nightmarish privilege of leading the British Open with one day remaining.

He could tell himself that this was a moment for jubilation and he had acted the part for his public knowing that he would be frightened, when they had all departed, to be left alone with this lead and the immense burden it placed upon him.

It had all been easy until this moment. He had come to Portrush brimming with confidence and possessed of a fearless determination that he could win although he never voiced that feeling. And it had been easy in that way to attack the course in cavalier fashion during those early rounds, because the title seemed far off and the championship without shape.

Now it had settled, he was alone at the front of the field, and the hardest part of this championship was to endure that night, that limbo, alone with his lead as though time had stood still, and he was paralysed, except for his mind, which was left to contemplate the dreadful alternatives.

He had thought that his customary wade through the foam along the sea shore might have helped as it had done on the previous evenings after dinner. But this time it offered no relaxation. And he thought about Stranahan, the American, and how he had summed up the next day's situation when everybody would charge towards Faulkner knowing that this self-acknowledged clown of British golf had found himself, by some curious mishap, in the lead, and how easy it would be to remove him.

Stranahan had bawled out his challenge as they left the dining-room of the Great Northern Hotel in Portrush that night. He was eight strokes behind Faulkner, yet claimed that it was not such a great gap to close over two rounds.

Faulkner had been stung into quick retaliation, yet it was more than this that made him call the American to one side and insist that he did not speak to Faulkner throughout the next day when they would be paired together. Faulkner was not so much concerned about Stranahan's golf as his loud talk and what that could do to Faulkner's own concentration.

The American had seemed surprised and hurt at the request, since he accepted Maxie as the outrageous extrovert of British golf, the man who wore pink plus fours and matching shoes, who begged the world to laugh at him. Here he was now, asking to be taken seriously.

Faulkner had come to Portrush that week knowing, yet not daring to disclose, that he felt a growing expectancy about this championship. He had joked with Rees and Bousfield about who was going to be second, but only because they expected that kind of wisecrack from him.

He had played well all season and he was feeling extremely fit. His putting was in the midst of an inspired spell brought on, he was convinced, by the old putter he had discovered in Henry Cotton's shop at Royal Mid-Surrey.

While it was true that after he had bent, filed and lengthened this putter, the very sight of the club gave him more confidence on the green, he knew that this magic had only a limited life. His attic at home was filled with discarded putters whose magic had been dissipated.

How could one club – that special club – transform his golf? Surely it was the man and not the club? Every club in his attic had felt right for a moment and suddenly, for some unfathomable reason, it had assumed the grace of a sledge hammer and been thrown away – but not quite, since there was always the hope that the magic might return.

It was senseless, this belief that there was a putter waiting somewhere that would cure all ills, that would protect his imperfections, banish his doubts and, of its own accord, make him play well. Maybe it was a necessary deception to ease the awesome burden of a livelihood which depended daily on the turn of a ball into a hole.

It would be Faulkner, not his putter, who would be called upon to defend a three-stroke lead over that final day. He could not hide behind the hope that somehow these pieces of iron and wood would play more than their share – take some of his part – in that task. They were implements in his hands and could do no more than he allowed them.

Did he have the will power to prevail over everybody for a full day? He was convinced he did not have the proper temperament. He was too quick, too excitable, and boxing or football, any activity demanding reflex action was more his style.

Gus, his father, had always announced him even in childhood as a future Open champion and now Faulkner was saddled with the task of determining whether Gus's dearest wish could be become reality.

His golf he knew was good enough. But he was uncertain whether he possessed the strength of purpose to endure. After all, he was a man who could not give up smoking cigarettes even though he knew that he should. And then a small thought struck him. He would give up cigarettes for the day as though this would be a constant reminder to him that his will power was functioning. It would also keep his head clear, but that was not quite so convincing an argument, since he had got this far, to the front of the field, with his perpetual cigarette smoking.

But why should he be afraid? He was playing well. He was fit. He was three strokes clear. He could cope with Portrush. Why should he worry now? If he looked back, the memories were good. The future would be no different. Of course he was going to win. It was waiting there for him at the end of the day. He opened his eyes and it was daylight. He must have been asleep for a little while at least.

Stranahan was first on the tee, and when Faulkner ducked through the ropes and greeted him, the American turned away. Faulkner had laid the ground rules on the previous night and Stranahan was to observe them to the letter.

As soon as Faulkner began to play, the butterflies deserted his stomach and he knew, really knew, that no matter how many bad strokes he played that day, he would emerge as champion. It was a feeling of enormous strength and confidence that he was never able to explain. He felt caught up by a spirit and power greater than himself, and that day he demonstrated many times that he was, as it were, simply the instrument of this greater force.

By the side of the eleventh green, he was trapped in a deep bunker with the flagstick perched virtually on its edge, and it was as though he had to play the ball up the side of a brick wall and land on the top. He did it without fuss, as though he knew it would happen.

The sixteenth hole in that morning round showed the curious contradiction that is part of a champion's character;

fallible enough to be distracted into a bad stroke by a stray thought, yet composed and determined enough to escape brilliantly from the subsequent crisis.

Faulkner already knew there was no challenge coming from the field, and that steady golf back to the clubhouse now would give an insurmountable lead. The thought was a distraction he should never have permitted because as he pulled the driver back towards the ball, his muscles tightened and he knew the sequence was wrong. But it was too late to stop. The ball tore away to the left, and on towards the out-of-bounds fence.

Before it landed, Faulkner knew that it was safe and would not break through the out-of-bounds fence. It was not a judgement of the stroke, but more this conviction that nothing would go badly wrong for him; that no crisis would be too disastrous; that nobody else was directed by the same kind of force.

The ball was a yard in play from the barbed wire fence. There was still much of the hole left to play, but a wooden club seemed impossible since a full backswing would be trapped by the fence. A gentle nudge with his wedge would put the ball on the fairway and give him the chance to attack with his third stroke.

But Faulkner felt compelled to aim for the green, not because he was afraid that news of this trouble might spark somebody else into action, but because he had that special greed of a man for whom nothing can go wrong.

He reached for his spoon and edged his backside gently against the barbed wire. The club was gripped down the shaft and not only would he have to chop down on the ball to escape the fence, but he would also have to aim down the length of the fence and hope to impart enough spin on the ball to bring it away from the trouble and in towards the green.

Faulkner knew that he would acquire more slice if he aimed towards the out of bounds and, at the same time, that it would give him the luxury of a fractionally longer backswing. The crowd watched in horror as this man with the Open championship virtually in his pocket, aimed with calculated recklessness off the course.

He steadied himself and waited for the moment when his swing would spring into life almost of its own accord. The club jarred pleasingly in his hands and told him that he had made good contact with the ball. Then he saw it, flying along the line of the fence as if dithering about which way to turn.

It seemed an eternity before it made up its mind, then began to drift away from the fence and in towards the green. Faulkner could tell from the flight of that ball that there was still enough power in it to reach the green and then, in the corner of his eye, he caught sight of the flag and knew that the ball was on perfect course.

Delighted cheers greeted the ball as it screwed into the green a few feet from the hole. Even Stranahan broke his vow of silence to applaud, and tell Faulkner it was the greatest golf stroke he had ever seen. In that moment both he and Faulkner knew that the championship was over.

They lunched together, the American nibbling at his food while Faulkner demolished one plate of steak and kidney pie then asked for another. Faulkner was completely at ease, yet he summoned his caddie and walked away to the practice ground to await the start of that final round.

He did not need the practice, but he had to avoid people and the idle moment when he might dwell of this last round. He remembered how Cotton had made this kind of mistake at Royal St. George's in 1934 and had put himself through unnecessary agonies.

Faulkner was now six strokes clear, with one round left, and he permitted himself one presumption as he walked to the tee and signed his autograph: 'Max Faulkner, 1951 Open champion'. His last round was an object lesson in discreet play and even though the Argentinian, Cerda made a late charge, Faulkner was out of reach. He was champion by two strokes.

He came off the last green and realised that he had not smoked all day. He asked Rees for a cigarette but the Welsh-man did not have one. They reached the Pressmen and a cigarette was found. On his second puff, Faulkner went dizzy and almost passed out. But by the end of that evening, he had made up his daily quota, and was able to cope with nicotine again.

Chapter 14: *World Match Play Final, Wentworth, 1967*

Even as Palmer spoke, the words seemed wrong, because they expressed a sentiment nobody suspected he possessed. It was beneath him, something much less than the image they had of him. He had been the hero for so many reasons, but not until that moment, when he spoke, did anybody realise how much he had been loved for his magnificent arrogance which disregarded others as he focused on a personal contest with the golf course.

It had meant, of course, that he never showed malicious regard for others, since they were unimportant at the time. That was part of his appeal. But all that changed with those words or perhaps Palmer himself had changed, because now he had indulged in the kind of intimidating repartee, before this World Match Play final, that was more typical of heavy-weight fighters.

It was not quite so boorish, but its impact was just as great, since he had never hinted at such thoughts before. He told the Pressmen : 'I always like to win. But I guess you can say that we Americans take particular pleasure in beating Peter.'

Thomson was his target even before this final had started, because he knew the Press would report it and that it would probably get back to Thomson. The statement contained so many calculated threats and cloaked insults that it was hard at first to believe that Palmer, of all people, had uttered it. There had been some mutual disdain, but everybody had assumed that it was more deeply felt by Thomson, who made no secret of his dislike of American values but who had never narrowed his sights to Palmer in particular. But now Palmer had assumed the role of champion of the American cause, and fired the first blast before the match started.

Why was Palmer thus provoked? Why had he descended from his magnificent isolation to join the rest of the human race in a bout of pettiness? What kind of man was this Thomson to evoke such thoughts, since apart from a T.V. match, he had never really humiliated Palmer on a golf course; nor in the separate worlds in which they moved did either man affect the other?

Thomson's general derogatory remarks about American golf could never have bitten that deeply into Palmer, since the American had collected more major titles throughout the world and had amassed a personal business empire that left no doubt about who had made the greater success of professional golf.

And this was more than the instant hate which every professional directs at an opponent. What each disliked in the other was not altogether personal, since they did not know each other that well. But each disliked what the other stood for; the processes which had given each a lasting, but totally different, place in golf history. Neither was absolutely certain which had the greater merit, and this wrankled.

They were alien to each other in manner and attitudes. Their common ground was a golf course, but even here they adopted such contrasting attitudes as if engaged in different subjects. Thomson could see in Palmer a man for whom the wider repertoire of a champion had not been necessary, because of a consummate ability of combining power and a deftness around and on the greens.

Thomson could appear as a half-formed champion, a man who stopped halfway up the ladder because he was not capable of going higher; a man who had shown suspicious selectivity in his competitive play even though the true champion should be able to take on and beat all-comers anywhere.

They were the same age, born into totally differing attitudes towards the playing of golf. Palmer, the son of a professional, had seen himself fitted for no other life. Thomson, a man of much broader intellectual range, had been launched on a scientific career before turning to professional golf. Thomson drew pleasure from a concert of classical music or the ponderous biography of some statesman. This kind of stuff never appealed to Palmer. Nor could he escape his public image to find the freedom which Thomson enjoyed.

Not that the facility to go unnoticed had ever bothered Palmer overmuch, since he thrived on acclaim and was lost without it. But this freedom in Thomson presented itself as part of a self-sufficiency which added to his air of irritating and, to Palmer, ill-founded, superiority.

Were Thomson's five British Opens, plus a few other things won in quiet corners of the world, worth more than the fifty titles that he, Palmer, had accumulated in the furnace of American professional golf (where Thomson had burned his fingers so badly)? Palmer had won wherever the airliner set him down. Who had the greater talent?

Their golf philosophies kept them at extremes because Palmer gave the impression that a hole could be crushed with overwhelming power and a sure touch with a putter. Thomson, with no such power at his disposal, tackled a golf course with more apparent planning, and needed to exert his skill on the ball to find his chosen spots on each fairway. Thomson, it seemed, charted his route, while Palmer roared along a path of his own choice and making.

To Thomson, judgement was as important as skill, and he detested the artificiality of American courses, with their watered greens and tailored rough, because judgement had departed from that kind of golf, and it had been reduced to dart-board targetry. Thomson's arguments were weakened by his lack of success in the United States. But he remained, nonetheless, critical of their attitude and wondered at times how these men whose campaign plans were written in their notebooks after hours of rehearsal would fare if, just once, nobody was allowed on a golf course until the first round of a tournament. That, to Thomson, was the essential art of golf; an ability to sense and then adapt to changing conditions. By his definition, this was golf, and to remove any or all of these features was to call it by another name.

It would be impossible to prove anything of significance in a thirty-six-hole final, yet for each man there would be some personal satisfaction in triumph over the other, and Palmer's remarks had made it clear that more than just the first prize and a winner's blazer was at stake.

The next day, heavy with a chilling greyness, captured the grim mood of both men as they arrived on the first tee of Wentworth's West Course. Palmer bristled impatiently like a race horse, while Thomson's leisured manner, mirrored the apparent smugness which Palmer and other Americans found so irritating. Neither made the slightest concession to ease the mood by a hint of geniality, and as they set off down the valley towards the first hole, it seemed that this was a conflict between two philosophies, two differing skills, within the game.

The furious determination of their play showed just how much it mattered; they launched stroke after stroke at each other, but found there was always an adequate answer. Palmer allowed his man to get away from him, but then reeled him back with the confidence of an expert fisherman. At lunchtime they were still level.

Thomson, however, had more on which to ponder, since he had lost his lead to a blistering counter-attack by the American over the finishing holes, and it was an admission to Palmer that, if Thomson was pushed that hard down the same stretch in the afternoon, he might buckle again.

But the inflexible pattern endured into the afternoon, with furious activity and outstanding strokes – but none of them was decisive enough to establish a clear advantage. Both men, it seemed, had found an equal and opposite force, and both began to fear that there was nothing extra within himself that could shape the outcome.

Each was pouring out all his resources of skill, experience and energy, but this was not enough. Neither would budge an inch, and while this stubbornness displayed their skills, it was based in a burning, gut-twisting pride that makes this kind of man prefer to lose an arm rather than a match.

With nine holes left, they were still level, with both playing to their limits. Then, quite suddenly, Palmer erupted. At first there had been no hint of the volcanic savagery of his attack when he drilled his tee shot over the trees of the short tenth, within a few feet of the hole, for a birdie two.

To Thomson it was an acceptable, and not intimidating fluctuation in the game. But something had transformed Palmer. Time was running out, and this compelling urgency was the catalyst for the change. All day it had not mattered, but now, as they trailed back to the clubhouse, Palmer was losing the luxury of time and had to act fast.

He unleashed a savage blow over the trees and far into the distance of the long twelfth hole, and he knew, the moment he connected, the ball would be far enough down that fairway for him to grab the green with his next blow while Thomson might be stretched to reach the front edge.

It was a blow of superb calculation, since it also reminded Thomson that power would certainly decide the longer finishing holes, and that he himself might, before long, be forced to hang on to Palmer's pace rather than dictate the terms.

The American seized his chance joyfully, and thrashed the ball with all his strength towards the far-away green. Long before the cheers, he knew that it was a good stroke, and the black speck moved towards the waiting flagstick.

When they reached the green both men saw that Palmer's ball was so close to the hole that he had earned himself an automatic eagle three, and if this was the fruit of power, then it needed no apology. Thomson was two down.

Now it was beginning to take shape and Thomson's faith

in the par-fours, where he could match Palmer, was badly shaken on the thirteenth, when the American's approach shot almost trickled into the hole. Thomson was three down.

They had not looked at each other during this skirmish, because neither wanted to give anything away to the other by such a look – particularly Palmer, who wanted to be sure that he did not let Thomson see how much it all mattered. But, anyway, Thomson was too locked within his own thoughts to have noticed.

Palmer did not underestimate Thomson, not now, after the manner in which they had toiled all day, but that inspired burst had always been an essential part of Palmer's play, an automatic part of the process of winning, and a clear sign to himself that triumph was inevitable.

Thomson was far too preoccupied to be influenced by such portents, and made a token thrust by winning back the short fourteenth up the hill with a birdie two. He suspected, as he stood on the next tee, that Palmer, with all his power, might find the trees just a little claustrophobic, and decide against hitting a big drive between them.

Palmer did ease off, and found himself with no clear advantage from the tee. Suddenly, it was Thomson who struck an immense blow to the heart of the green, and the explosive strength of the blow surprised Palmer, who yielded to an eagle three, so that there was only one hole between them. Now Thomson was dictating the terms, and when he struck an unerring approach into the sixteenth green Palmer had shown his growing tiredness with an inaccurate iron, which left the ball a long way from the hole on that green.

Here the match could be levelled, and Palmer's resolution torn to shreds as he realised he had given away a three-hole lead in the dying minutes of the match.

This was the moment when all the failures of the past would crowd in upon Palmer as he stood over that long putt that had to drop for a birdie if he was to save his lead.

This was when he would fight the improbability of its success, and the pressure, and his body. This was the real test that they had taken all day to find.

Palmer crouched over his ball, knees locked, head low and shoulders hunched. The crowd watched and wondered whether this man could really believe that he could guide a ball over that tortuous terrain into a hole that was barely visible. He must know that Thomson would win this match if he failed now.

He was locked there for what seemed an eternity, then, the calculations complete, the putter angled for good or bad, he had to commit himself to a stroke. Suddenly it was on its way, and by the time the ball had covered half the distance, the crowd knew that it had sufficient pace.

If he had judged the subtleties of that green correctly, then the ball had a fighting chance. Then he knew, even with the ball a long way from the hole, that it had found the perfect route into the hole. The cheering reached a savage shriek as it disappeared into the depths.

Still Palmer did not look at Thomson, but instead acknowledged the cheers. Thomson marched through the noise to his own ball. What Palmer had endured, he must now face. Fate had decided it seemed, that both should face the absolute test on this green, and though Palmer's putt had been longer, Thomson's test was more critical, since he was putting against the fact of Palmer's success, while the American, moments earlier, had only suspicion to urge him. This now was an act of survival for Thomson when only seconds ago, it had seemed nothing more than a ritual towards triumph. If he missed, he too was finished.

He took a few practice strokes, shuffled stiff-legged to the ball, and knew that Palmer was watching it all with eased relief. Thomson, his hands high on the club, seemed frozen by the pressures of that moment.

And then the clubhead moved gently back, so slowly there was time to count on the backswing, and the ball moved forward and again the cheers split that grey afternoon as it, too, disappeared from sight.

But Palmer still held his one-hole lead; Thomson had made his last effective thrust and it had failed. The encounter was already finished, yet it endured formally to the last green. When it was over, Thomson walked across the green to shake hands with Palmer, the winner.

They looked at each other for a moment, and it was not an unseeing stare yet whatever emotion each man felt, remained unsaid. Maybe it had just been the instinctive reaction of one professional to another, a fleeting acknowledgement of the other's fight. But whatever it was, it remained the true feeling, and not to be confused with the platitudes that each would expound later.

Thomson said simply: 'I was beaten by a better man.' Palmer had won the match but that victory had gained in importance because of Thomson's judgement of it. They always listened to what Thomson said. Nothing had changed that day – save for that fleeting look of respect on the last green. That, too, would soon be forgotten.

Chapter 15: *The Ryder Cup, Royal Birkdale, 1969*

Not far down Waterloo Road, the traffic halted, then crawled on towards the course. But Snead hardly noticed, because there were more urgent matters to capture his attention. He had brought an invincible team to Southport to contest the Ryder Cup. Even the names were already part of golf history – Nicklaus, Trevino, Casper, Littler – and the others were not exactly beginners.

By now, on this last day, he should be thinking about his speech, and finding a new way of telling the same old lie about how close this match had been with the British and how much they had improved. But this time, he could ill afford the presumption of thoughts about a speech. In the past two days his men had done nothing to prove they were the best in the world. They were still locked evenly with the British team, most of whom were unknown to him.

For that reason he had geniune cause to worry. He knew, in all modesty, that there was not a better collection of golfers on the planet Earth than his team – and yet a bunch of 'faceless' Britishers refused to admit it!

He could see, sensibly, that on this day of singles his men held all the advantages because they were accustomed to success, and if they had been shackled by the obligations of foursomes and then fourball golf, now they could play more comfortably for themselves in the manner of their professional life. Yet Snead knew from his own experience that it could never be quite like that – that at the back of each mind would be the nagging awareness of the implications of every stroke.

It was all true, but the situation still augured better for his men, because this Ryder Cup mattered too much to the British, and dominated their thinking. It was easy enough to bang drums and make rousing speeches – but did they have the guts to reach out when they were close?

The British side had no pedigree worth talking about. There was Jacklin, of course, and he had won the British Open that summer. But even he could not be ranked with Nicklaus and his small coterie of distinguished golfers. And anyway, one man cannot make a team. How and why, then, were they still holding out?

Had their captain Eric Brown really been able to drill some fresh spirit into them? Could he forge them into a cohesive force in such a short time? Could he stand back from that familiarity to appear before them as an inspired dictator?

Snead doubted it, but something must have happened. Brown had set the mood for this contest early in the week when he declared that his men would not assist any American to look for his golf ball in the rough. The real intention of his statement had been to issue a clear-cut warning that this time the British would not smile meekly all the way to defeat.

There had been the business over the shrinking tees, and the rumours that a couple of holes would be altered to suit the weather conditions, and that only the British would know if that switch took place. What rubbish! That was easy to check and yet again, the aim had been to make his men aware of the hostile atmosphere into which they had stepped.

None of it should have been unsettling, but the antagonism had touched some of them, and Ken Still had shown the strain by losing his temper in a fourball match against Brian Huggett and Bernard Gallacher. The crowd had booed him and his partner Dave Hill. It had been an awful error of judgement. You never win when you take on the crowd.

Hills and Still should never have sulked, and certainly not conceded the hole just because Huggett pointed out to the referee that the Americans had played out of turn. And then to attempt to claim the eighth hole from Gallacher and Huggett. God Almighty!

It had been a justified if over-zealous tactic by Gallacher to concede Still's return putt because Hill was in the same area of the green and could learn much from the way Still's ball broke across the contours. Still knew the reason, and made a pathetic attempt to claim the hole. Then, when that failed, he took on the crowd.

For the rest of that round, he was a marked man. The crowd cheered when his ball landed in a bunker, and policemen were hurried out to calm the mood while Nicklaus, Littler and some of the others tried to placate Still and his partner, who were in a highly emotional state. It had been a painful revelation for Nicklaus, hailed as the second Messiah whenever he appeared in Britain, to realise that this time he was here on different terms, and that he was part of the invading force.

Perhaps if there had been more daylight at the end of those marathon fourball matches, the Americans might have been ahead. Certainly Trevino's Scottish caddie would not have slipped and broken his leg as they walked to the last tee, but more important, Trevino or Barber might have holed their shortish putts on the final green for the point that would have given his team a lead.

Now Snead must wait and hope that the individual talents of his men could assert themselves, and he was certain that he had set his team out correctly. Trevino was top and Nicklaus was in last place, with Casper somewhere in the middle.

Trevino could beat anybody Brown liked to select as an opener, and Nicklaus would pick up an easy point or at least forestall any hopes that Brown might have of a soft touch that low in the batting order. In fact both captains had thought the same about last place, yet it worried Snead very little because he was convinced that Nicklaus, Trevino and Casper must be winners, and that their example would influence the rest of his men, so that although victory might take a little longer this year, there was no doubt about it.

By lunchtime he was not so sure, and the nightmare had begun to take shape of his getting off the plane after the return journey at the head of the strongest golf team in the world which he had led to defeat. Even Jackie Burke back in 1957 had a reasonable excuse that he had not been given the best golfers. Snead had no such escape clause.

In another part of Royal Birkdale's clubhouse Eric Brown could not resist a smile because his boys had opened a two-point lead, and the greatest boost to the morale of his side had come from Jacklin, who had annihilated Nicklaus. This news spread around the course, and lifted his team into uninhibited aggression.

What pleased Brown even more was that he had two of his strongest players, completely fresh, to throw into the afternoon struggle for the minimum three-and-a-half points that Britain needed for victory. Gallacher and Huggett would certainly be needed now, and he was glad that he had rested them.

Both had proved themselves to be in peak form, and because of that, not the least frightened by the Americans nor their personal tasks. But Brown knew that it was to be a close finish, and again wanted his steady men low in the order. Jacklin was still in the tail-end, with Coles just in front of him and trailing Huggett.

Whatever else, Snead was not going to win this 'from the back', and Brown's strategy had seemed to work well enough when, once again, Jacklin drew Nicklaus at the end of the list with Huggett facing Casper, while towards the front Gallacher had emerged against Trevino, a man whom he had already beaten in an exhibition match.

But Brown knew that it was impossible to guess what hidden incentives of pride would now begin to work for these Americans as they realised they were fighting for their lives. And perhaps, for the first time that week, all of the Americans had been touched by and made painfully aware of the greater responsibility now upon them as a national team, which demanded even greater effort than they could ever muster for themselves.

Brown knew that the pressure would increase on his own men as they realised how close they had come to the unattainable. But would that apprehension show in their golf at a time when the Americans must cut loose viciously? Each stage was harder than the one just passed, and there was no consolation in remembering what his boys had done for the last few days. It was a new, more exhaustive examination each time they played. None of them would have experienced anything as extreme as this last afternoon. He could only wait and hope.

On the last afternoon of an international match, the Press room takes on the atmosphere of base headquarters during a battle. From there it is possible to see the battle take shape, to see one side advancing and the other in retreat. Once the pattern has been set, it is then possible to move into the field for first-hand knowledge of the conflict.

So it was that afternoon, as the scoreboard began to chart the path of a blistering American counter-attack, in which the British lead was devoured and more casualties were reported. The fighting was vicious, as the British had expected, and now they feared that the Americans would swamp them.

Each man in Brown's team looked around for inspiration, for the slightest sign that at least one of them was standing firm. Cometh the hour, cometh the man or in this case, the boy. Gallacher, like the heroic drummer boy, marched through the mayhem and the casualties in relentless pursuit of Lee Trevino. And so ruthlessly was the angelic-faced Scot achieving his task that for once Trevino found nothing about which to smile. Gallacher damaged him badly, and gave Brown his first point of that afternoon. Peter Butler followed with customary humdrum brilliance. Now they needed, at worst, only one-and-a-half points to deliver the trophy back to Britain.

But Brown's men had sustained heavy losses, and soon there were only two men left standing – Jacklin and Huggett. By the sixteenth hole the tenacious, grim-faced Welshman was still square with Casper. Behind him, Jacklin trailed one down to Nicklaus, and this seemed sadly predictable, because it is hard to beat the same man twice in one day, and virtually impossible when that man is Jack Nicklaus.

Huggett was then under the impression that Jacklin was all square with Nicklaus, and this misapprehension brought a more burdensome light on his own task – one of them had to win, and the other scrape at least a half point.

Yet both had to prevail against two of the most accomplished golfers in the world if they were to succeed in earning the trophy. To the crowds who watched, no two British golfers were better equipped for that task. Jacklin had limitless ability, particularly in front of his home crowd, and the British Open triumph a few months earlier had boosted his confidence. Huggett was different – but equally well fitted to his task.

His class and skill came through dogged determination and experience, and what Huggett had achieved with his life had been fought for all the way. He fought his small stature, his difficulties with the larger-sized golf ball, the doubts of others that almost invaded his own belief. He was a terrier who would never let go, and he had shown this in two previous British Opens. At the very worst, Brown was certain to get a half-point from Huggett, and they both knew it.

Huggett's stomach was a tight as a knot, and it always happened like this under tension. In a way he wished it would end now, but knew that for that to happen he would have to lose, because certainly Casper was not going to yield.

The Welshman knew that he must live with the pain a

little longer, and if Casper seemed removed from it all, as if enjoying an afternoon stroll, then Huggett knew this was not the truth. Casper had confessed during the 1967 Ryder Cup match that he felt very nervous during these matches because it was not just himself who would suffer by failure.

That was how it was, as they played the long seventeenth, yet Casper had this champion's gift of freeing his swing from inhibiting tension so that it worked at its normal superior efficiency. And he jammed his third stroke close to the flag-stock, while Huggett, five feet from the hole, knew that he would have sweat his way to halve the hole.

But he had expected this – that he would find himself countering Casper's moves, and he preferred it, since it meant that he never ventured into the unknown, but simply answered the reality that Casper produced.

His face was drawn tight-lipped with jaw-jutting concen-tration as he hovered over the ball, while Casper looked around in apparent disinterest at the intolerable strain he had applied to a fellow human being. Huggett had peered at the ball from all sides like a man examining an unexploded bomb. Then he was ready. He eased the putter back then looked quickly as the ball moved towards the hole and was devoured. Casper had not broken clear.

By the time they reached the last green Huggett found himself with a remote chance to end it all, because he was thirty feet from the hole and would have to strike the ball hard to counteract the slower pace of the green, caused by the rain which had fallen in the last few minutes. And if he was compelled to hit hard, then he might just as well attack the hole instead of lagging the putt close enough for the safety of the next one. It was to be a departure from his strategy – a step into the unknown.

It was not really his style because it is not possible to gauge strength and precise direction from that sort of dist-ance, but he forced the ball some four feet past the hole and knew that, once again, he would have to work hard to save his point.

The next moment was to change his life; it took him to a new peak of achievement and established him among the truly courageous sporting heroes. There was an ecstatic roar from the seventeenth green, frightening in its suddenness and so prolonged as to mean only one awesome thing to Huggett. Jacklin had beaten Nicklaus and the Ryder now rested on this putt which he was about to play.

Huggett felt sure that the roar meant triumph for Jacklin. A professional learns to 'read' the roars of the crowds because they can tell him so much about people's fortune, and this one had been too long, loud and hysterical for anything but triumph.

Huggett was now the most important golfer on Earth, and about to play a stroke that would be remembered for ever. The pain was still there in his guts, and there were thousands around that green – yet their very silence seemed oppressive.

The putt was not difficult to read; it was straight, with no tricks, and he had stood over and holed thousands of putts of this length – but never of this importance. His mind began to calculate, as if by instinct, that there might be a great temptation to underhit this ball because of this frightening moment and because his last memory was of the preceding putt which had been too strong.

How awful to let a putt of perfect line die in the mouth of the hole. Then he resolved that the longer he thought the more difficult this putt would become. Huggett struck the ball and his eyes flicked to the left to watch it make the journey. It was on perfect line and nothing could stop it. It rolled, and rolled and rolled, centred itself on the hole, then vanished. Huggett punched the air in relief and turned to find Casper.

The crowd erupted but Huggett did not hear them, for in

that moment he stood bewildered like a man roughly awakened. He scanned the crowd for a familiar face, saw Eric Brown, who rushed forward. Suddenly Huggett was in tears. It was too early for joy, yet he wept as the tension flowed from him.

Brown embraced him like a consoling father, and the rest of us blinked back the tears, and not because Huggett would learn in a few moments of his error, and that he had not won the Ryder Cup for his country. That did not seem to matter. Huggett's tears captured the intensity of the race Brown's team had run, and showed just how much they had given of themselves to the task. Our tears were for the sheer magic of that moment, that unrepeatable point in time. Huggett had nothing left to give. Nobody had given more.

The roar from the seventeenth, as he would soon learn, had not signalled Jacklin's victory, but was just an expression of sheer delight as Jacklin brazenly holed an eagle putt the length of the green to draw level with Nicklaus as they went to the last fairway. Now both were on that final green, each knowing for certain that the Ryder Cup rested on these closing minutes. Yet few people among those thousands wanted either man to lose – especially these two – for the stigma would so gravely and disproportionately weigh against their great talents.

This battle had been too closely fought with honest endeavour to belong to either side, and certainly too finely balanced to be decided now by a putt. Maybe Brown, Snead, Hill and Still were blind to the injustice of anything but a tie. And perhaps it is the weakness in we British – this damaging sense of justice that makes a batsman walk even when the umpire did not see – but it is a way as good as any other.

Jacklin was first to putt, and the crowd thanked the Almighty – and Brown's shrewdness – that this weight of responsibility had fallen on the strongest shoulders in the

GREAT MOMENTS IN SPORT : GOLF

British team. In the absolute crunch it was Jacklin, our man but trained in their ways, who had the job.

His putt from the back of the green halted two feet from the hole, and now he had to wait while Nicklaus attempted to finish him off and win the Ryder Cup with his own putt. Nicklaus was only fifteen feet from the hole, a distance he is inclined to regard as guaranteed for a certain putt.

But the pressure had found its way into Nicklaus's concentration, and the speed with which he struck that putt declared openly that he was only too aware of the burden placed upon him. This was his first Ryder Cup, and already he was enduring a deep obligation to something beyond his own reputation.

His ball finished four feet away on the other side of the hole, and it was still his turn to putt. This would indeed be a tragedy if this great golfer, perhaps the greatest in history, now failed with the last putt of the last match on the last green – that this great contest should now be decided by an error.

Jacklin wanted to win, but not this way – yet Nicklaus was too far away to concede that putt. The crowd knew it, too, even though they prayed that Nicklaus would not fail. He took infinite care then coaxed the ball into the hole, and the crowd erupted in delight, then halted as they remembered that Jacklin still had to sink his own putt to save the series.

Then they realised that Nicklaus was smiling, hand outstretched towards Jacklin. Nicklaus had conceded the putt and said: 'I didn't think you would miss it – but I wasn't going to give you the chance!'

His decision allowed the Ryder Cup to be tied (for while it is fairly certain that Jacklin would have holed, the fact is that he did not). But Nicklaus, too, had been touched by the appalling injustice that would have come from Jacklin's failure at that moment.

The two men clung to each other's shoulders as they walked from the last green, and the crowd roared approval, partly because Britain had not lost, partly because of the excitement of the British fight, but mostly because they had seen the most gifted golfers in the world driven to their limits for glory – not cash.

Chapter 16: *Bill Casper, Olympic, San Francisco, 1966*

When the news reached Petaluna, the brethren of the Church of Jesus Christ and Latter Day Saints rejoiced – then realised it meant they had to find another speaker for the evening meeting. Elder Casper, and his colour slides of Vietnam, must be out, because the word from Olympic, an hour's drive north, was that he had dared to stand in Arnold Palmer's way as the great man was about to win the U.S. Open championship, and had forced him to an eighteen-hole play-off the next day.

Whatever happened tomorrow, Casper would now need the solitude, or the freedom to come to terms with that fresh encounter with Palmer. It would be too much to expect him to endure the distractions and the journey that would rob him of this valuable time.

They were still pondering on a replacement when the message came from Casper that he would arrive at the Californian church as promised, then would drive back to Olympic to catch a few hours sleep.

It seemed a magnificent gesture, and if not quite self-sacrifice, then at least a commendable generosity of spirit in that he could honour his obligations at a moment when the greatest prize in his life was available the next day and should have occupied his thoughts. But to Casper, the gesture to continue had not been that generous, and constituted his part of a monumental bargain he had struck with God at a moment of revelation during that afternoon's struggle in the final round with Palmer.

With nine holes of that championship left to be played,

Casper had no ambitions. This was Palmer's day and his own personal concern was whether anybody could threaten him for second place. It was Palmer who told him not to worry about it.

Palmer was so far ahead, seven strokes clear, that it was pointless even thinking that he could be caught now. Yet another championship had passed Casper by although in fairness Palmer had collared this one by the throat early on, and had warned everybody that this was to be his possession. Casper wanted another title because the paradox of his life was that he could make a million dollars and head a giant business based on his golf skill, yet he could not capture the major titles with the frequency that his talent demanded. It mattered to him because it mattered to others.

Only once had he captured a worthy title – the U.S. Open – and even then it had been suggested that his phenomenal putting and little else had achieved it. And the demands on a one-time winner grow even more oppressive and urgent as he endeavours to win again to prove that the first time was not just a lucky break. Casper still awaited that proof.

In the meantime he continued, a discontented man, inflating his bank balance by weekly triumphs yet finding little satisfaction in it. He had what was called a money swing. It never went seriously wrong because it was geared to an unambitious steadiness which delivered him without incident to the green, where his considerable putting skill could function.

It was truly professional because it produced a weekly pay cheque and gave him a standard of living far beyond his dreams. He came from a broken home in California and this, together with the ensuing upheavals of various guardians, made him a withdrawn and slightly suspicious man.

He was fat, yet not even in his childhood was he the brunt of the ridicule sometimes directed at fat people. Casper had an exceptional deftness, a superb hand and eye co-ordination which made it possible for him to be more skilful in sports

155

such as tennis, baseball and golf than those around him. But this fatness in adult life brought with it a string of pestering minor ailments which made him ill-tempered and slightly neurotic. This was the background against which his disenchantment grew, as winning the ordinary events lost its meaning and the major championships seemed beyond his reach.

The Mormon faith came into his life at just the right moment, and he was to regard this itself as another sign of the Almighty's interest. His wife Shirley became interested in the faith during a tournament at Salt Lake City, the home of Mormonism. She adopted the faith, and Casper, brought up as a Catholic, eventually accepted it, too.

By coincidence he learned at this time of a doctor who maintained that some people were allergic to what seemed the most harmless foods – that these foods could have a poisonous effect which caused illness and even a fatness that had little to do with carbohydrate quotas.

Casper underwent tests and eliminated all those foods that had seemed harmless. He was left with a diet which included elk and buffalo meat, and he became so fussy that he would take his own food wherever he played. The Press gave him the nickname 'Buffalo Bill'. Casper saw the sense in it and used it as his trademark. He even opened a business selling 'buffalo-burgers'.

But the real importance of this anti-allergy treatment was that his weight reduced from 220 lb. to 180 lb., and the irritating ailments disappeared. Thus a new physique and a new spirit had come together. Through his faith, Casper found a new meaning to his life and saw his golf now as a vehicle by which he could spread the gospel. He undertook to give sermons and visit churches in whatever town he played.

His new religion demanded ten per cent of his considerable earnings, and Casper was happy enough to give it. Others doubted the depth of this 'Road to Damascus' con-

version and saw it as just another, if new, means of escape
for a tournament golfer from the black mood that invades
all of them from time to time.

Others drew similar solace and perhaps inspiration from
a bottle or a pretty face, but if it worked for Casper then
it could not be criticised. It was clear to everybody that
Casper had established a new working relationship with his
golf and that he now believed that it was an instrument of
God's work.

It seemed as though winning for its own sake lost importance, the attendant pressures on Casper were less and,
paradoxically, enabled him to win even more. But the championships were still out of reach and he was plagued by
a sense of injustice that although he had won as many tournaments as Palmer and more money than Player, he was considered an inferior talent because he could not match their
collections of major titles.

That day at Olympic gave him no cause for hope as he
walked alongside Palmer, now so utterly convinced of victory
that he had forgotten about it and was tempted to beat
Hogan's record Open aggregate which seemed the only challenge available to him.

Casper had forgotten that Palmer is at his weakest when
he appears to be unassailable. Palmer without a fight on
his hands is like a car without fuel, and cannot function.
Thus, his attempt on Hogan's record was not prompted by
greed but by a desperate need to find some pressure to bear
down on his game and make it work. Yet it was not real
enough to help him. This was his worst moment because
there was no immediate purpose for his golf.

His downfall began to take cruel shape on the short fifteenth at Olympic, across a gentle valley to a green protected by bunkers. The flagstick had been tucked behind the
bunkers on the right, but there was still a large expanse of
green to the left at which both men could aim. Neither suspected the remotest chance of change, even though Pal-

mer's lead had been reduced to five strokes with four holes left. Both knew that margin was adequate to see him home safely and even allow the luxury of a few errors.

Certainly Casper could not change his strategy of a lifetime and take chances. He would play, as he had always done, to the safe parts of the course, a stepping-stone tactic, which allowed his putter to work.

Thus he ignored the flagstick on the fifteenth because it was too well protected, and instead directed his tee shot with his seven-iron to the fat of the green on the left – allowing himself, at worst, two putts for his par-three.

But Palmer would not – could not – play that kind of percentage stroke, which deferred to the terrors of the hole. He saw only the flagstick because it was not in his nature to allow any golf course to dictate terms. In any case, he had attacked effectively all week and there was no reason to think that it would change for him now.

He ripped into his stroke with a seven-iron, trying to hold the ball out to the right and find the narrow space between flagstick and bunkers. But he had aimed too wide, and the ball dropped into a bunker. It was not serious, but when he blasted the ball fifteen feet past the hole he began to accept that he might drop a stroke to Casper. But that did not matter with so few holes left.

Casper moved to tackle his own long putt. He never dithers on the greens but acts in the manner of a man who is completely at home (and perhaps no golfer has ever spent more time on putting greens than Casper). This fact, which stemmed from his childhood, was not so much based on dedication as the understandable reluctance of a fat boy to exert himself by walking around a golf course in the San Diego heat.

Without fuss, he struck the ball on its intended line, aiming well left so that the slope of that green would bring the ball back to meet the hole. As he had guessed, the ball dropped from sight.

Casper had birdied the hole, and now Palmer's putt took on greater significance, because a failure would allow Casper to close the gap more than either had suspected possible. Some would maintain afterwards that this was the precise moment when the Palmer legend disintegrated. When Palmer missed that putt, it set off a chain reaction that was to cost him dearly – not only that day but over the ensuing years. Indeed, he was to finish that decade without another major title.

Casper was now only three strokes behind, and even though Palmer had won with this kind of margin and less many times, he was thinking negatively and was obsessed with what he had lost. Afterwards Casper remained convinced that Palmer panicked as they stood on the next tee and for the first time considered, however remotely, that it was possible for him to lose.

Palmer had known all week that it was suicide to take liberties with these tight fairways, yet he also realised that his only advantage over Casper on the extremely long sixteenth hole was his formidable power. With two of his best blows, Palmer could reach that green while Casper would need three hefty strokes to get home.

But, in his desperation to grab the distance, the swing was out of sequence and the ball blasted into life with no regard for the correct route. It fizzed low and left collided with a mass of trees within 200 yards of the tee and was buried. Casper moved safely into play and waited.

As Palmer picked his way carefully through the undergrowth he was filled with anxiety. This was the kind of hole, 604 yards, on which he should have dominated but now Casper, in the middle of the road, held all the advantages. Palmer should now clip that ball back to the fairway and from an even lie, thrash it towards the green and perhaps get home.

He would be level with Casper, who would need three

strokes to get there. But Palmer was now gripped in a panic that would not allow his discretion to work correctly. He could not give Casper any more hope.

Palmer saw enough daylight through the trees to suggest that there was a good chance that a really strong blow might break through. Even if the trees brought the ball down, it would have enough sting to give him more distance along the fairway. Anyway it was worth the risk. The alternative was to play the percentages – like a Casper.

His powerful hands wrapped around the club and he settled, with a curious animated stillness that promised thunderous revenge on that ball. He moved quickly, then unleashed all his fury at the ball – but the club never transmitted the message. The long grass drew its sting, turned the club in his hands and barely persuaded the ball to move a few yards.

Now he would be forced to accept the sanctions of this course and chip out meekly, as he should have done seconds ago. But even then the luck was running out, because, once he found the fairway again, his fourth stroke to that green trailed into a bunker.

Curiously this drama was still between Palmer and himself, with Casper the guiltless party, since he was playing no better and no worse than he did any day of the week. For that, he could not be blamed, but he turned the knife in Palmer's wound when he holed a long birdie putt on that hole. He had played it as Palmer knew he would – he even needed a full five-iron for his third stroke – yet he had delivered the ball into the hole with one putt.

Palmer sank miserably to a six, so that now there was only one stroke between them and the crowd was stunned to see the great Palmer lurching with indecision, for once a victim of the moment, when so often he had been its master.

It was then that Casper thought about God. It was part-demand, part-proposition. However impudent, he remembers trying to make God see the good sense of letting him win the U.S. Open since it would help in his missionary work.

That prayer, if such it was, held more conviction than hope, because Casper's own professional judgement of the situation told him that he held all the advantages now; that Palmer was losing to his own doubt and that the suddenness of it all – only twenty minutes ago both of them knew he would be champion – had robbed Palmer of his composure.

While Casper communicated with God, Palmer wrestled with the devil within himself and realised, in astonishment, that this Open, *his* Open, now rested on a man-to-man confrontation with Casper. That gave him cause for hope, since he still felt he could overwhelm Casper's instinctive caution and in any case, championships have to be won and not taken by default.

What he had overlooked was that his own monstrous tragedy had dwarfed the brilliance of Casper's play which was, by any standard, that of a winner. Both had a chance of a birdie on the seventeenth, but Palmer, playing slightly uphill, left his ball on perfect line but inches short of the hole. It was a sad admission that he, of all people, had not been bold enough when it mattered.

Casper stepped smartly to his own ball and tapped it across the green and into the hole. He had drawn level in just four holes, and Palmer was dumbfounded. This championship, which had been his for most of that week, was once again on the market.

Yet neither could capture it on the last hole, which they halved, and Palmer was grateful for the second chance. He felt he could beat Casper in a play-off. Yet Casper was now bolstered by something more than hope, and seemed already convinced how the next day would end.

Did Casper really get a heavenly nod? He remained convinced of it, though had to admit that as a professional of long experience he could see the inevitable path of Palmer's decline in that situation. Yet during that collapse the pressure had suddenly fallen upon Casper as he realised that Palmer could not save himself and the championship was available.

One thing is certain his own mind – he knew he was going to win after that seventeenth hole, and he had never had that kind of conviction through all his previous successes. Even though he had to pass that evening at Petaluna meeting fellow Mormons, he was certain what tomorrow would bring.

However, after nine holes that next day, he could be forgiven for thinking that the Lord works in mysterious ways. Palmer was two strokes clear, having shaken off the memories of his previous nightmare. Yet Casper kept the faith, and received the sign for which he waited on the eleventh hole, when his own ball bounced through rough to the green. Palmer tried the same route and was trapped. Casper birdied the hole but Palmer struggled for a six and they were even.

He finished Palmer before that round was over when he nailed a 30-footer across the thirteenth green for a birdie and thereby put himself into the lead of the U.S. Open for the first time. Palmer fell away angry and confused that he could no longer impose himself on events in the manner which he had patented.

Perhaps in that moment Palmer realised that he could no longer play like the thrusting dare-devilish Arnold of old – and yet, if there was consolation, then it was that it had taken a miracle to ruin him. Of that, Casper, at least was convinced.

They walked from that last green at Olympic with Casper the champion by four strokes. Palmer, head bowed, was shattered and on the point of tears. Even Casper could not smile. He rested a consoling arm on Palmer's shoulders as if the fall of this great champion took precedence over what was the greatest moment of his own career.

For not only had Casper joined the elite of great golfers who win a title twice, but he had outplayed the greatest golfer in the world at that time. Palmer had set new standards of golf by his own aggressive style, and Casper, because he could not copy that style, had never been given the accord he deserved. Not, at least, until that moment. Yet when these two styles were opposed, it was cool persistence and not inspirational brilliance which prevailed. In any case, inspiration is too unreliable. It never turned up the day Palmer needed it at Olympic.

Chapter 17: *The Ryder Cup, Lindrick, 1957*

Rees marched back into the dining-room feeling pleased with himself because he had been proved right, and because the others would be happy at his news. It was a small triumph, but at least it gave his team some hope and a reason to look forward with a little confidence towards the next day, instead of being afraid it would follow the predictable pattern of so many final days of Ryder Cup matches.

It had been a hard task to maintain his own enthusiasm at the team meeting, because this gloomy mood of acceptance seemed to hang over them as if they felt the hook in their gullets and knew that no amount of frenzied wriggling would free them.

The Americans had won the foursomes and such was their confidence that the day of singles that followed offered them no greater challenge than an exhibition match. What made the British mood so gloomy was that they had offered very little for the Americans to fight, and the score reflected British weakness rather than American strength.

Faulkner confessed to playing poor golf, and Brown, O'Connor, Alliss and Hunt had all played their parts in the failure. So had Weetman, and already this Ryder Cup was on its way home to the United States. The American captain Jackie Burke was sure of it, and so were his team.

Rees felt an angry frustration about it because he knew that this was not a strong American side, and that some of their best players – Snead, Demaret, and Middlecoff – had been left behind because they had not qualified through the correct number of tournaments. Burke's men had already been labelled by the U.S. Press as 'the weakest team ever to represent America', and yet even this depleted force seemed adequate enough to cope with the British effort.

If that label, or the traditional fallacy that Americans were unaccustomed to foursomes golf, had brought hope to British breasts, then it was deflated now as the Americans needed only four points for victory from that last day's singles matches.

Rees had conducted an inquest on the foursomes because he had not seen his men in action – he was otherwise engaged with Ken Bousfield in producing Britain's only winning point of the day against Art Wall and Fred Hawkins. He had decided that his team for the final day would be chosen by election rather than selection, and all of them had to help him because he refused to be a dictator.

His reasons for this process extended beyond the fact that he had not seen them play that day. These men were his colleagues for every week of the season except this one. Week after week they played, drank, dined and occasionally fought together. They knew each other too well, and Rees could not elevate himself out of their midst.

If this was a deficiency, then at least it was understandable. He could not remain aloof as Cotton had done, and order his men into monkish retreat and drill them like raw recruits. When the flags were lowered at Lindrick after this contest, Rees would be back among this crowd.

As captain he had to remain impartial to every member of his team, but as a working professional he had his preferences. And so this team by election was another means of remaining absolutely fair and, as he thought, beyond reproach. Whatever he thought of some of the others, it would not be seen, by this process, to have affected his judgement. All professionals on the tour acquire a measured tolerance of others because it is the only successful formula for life at close quarters. It is the barrack-room ethic, in that you may not like everyone in the billet but you learn to live and let live.

Rees, as a leader, became selfless yet exhaustively self-demanding for the cause. His own restless energy was turned towards producing the best in others. If it was still ego-inspired – *his* team and *his* reputation – then this did not matter, because the effect was good enough to outweigh the motive.

Few people really knew what drove Rees on, and even the Welshman himself, in his rare reflective moments, was not disposed to think about it overmuch. He hated to be alone, and would seek out company rather than endure a moment's solitude. He read books very rarely, and if others saw this need to be in a crowd as a deficiency, then perhaps for Rees it was an acceptance that this was his only means of identity, and he clung to it.

Maybe this was why, at that meeting, he hoped that the players themselves would suggest which of them did not play. Faulkner made it easy by saying that he should be dropped. That left one more name to be crossed off his list and he waited for a volunteer.

Weetman spoke up because he had played with Faulkner and must accept some of the blame, but Weetman could see, as others must, that the 4 and 3 defeat which they had suffered from Ted Kroll and Jackie Burke did not approach the abject failure of Eric Brown and Christy O'Connor, who had lost by 7 and 5.

Yet he, and the rest of those professionals in that room, knew the vagaries of the game, and knew that no matter how bad the golf had been today it could be transformed tomorrow for no other reason than it was a fresh start. The swing that creaked like a rusty pump handle one day could function with fluid ease the next.

Rees felt he had his consensus of opinion. Two of his most experienced professionals, Faulkner and Weetman, had admitted to poor golf and that was enough for him to tell them they were being dropped. Nobody seemed very surprised.

Next he had the more important task of piecing together his team in a manner to prevent an American win and, if they were as thinly spread as Rees suspected, perhaps even taking a decisive share of the last day singles. Rees needed a strong tail to his team because he felt that Burke, his counterpart, was not sure of a quick kill and would not open with his strong men in a decreasing order of ability. He would sprinkle them around the batting order.

Rees wrote down the names of the last three men – Bernard Hunt, Christy O'Connor and Harry Bradshaw. Hunt had already emerged as a strong competitor with a low-key temperament, but more important was Hunt's own memory of failure in his Ryder Cup debut at Wentworth, when his error on the last hole had contributed to the British loss. That still hurt deeply, and Rees knew that this young man would move heaven and earth to avoid defeat.

In that same Wentworth disaster, Harry Bradshaw, roly-poly genius of the short game, had prevailed as anchor man, even though it was a fruitless exercise. Rees gave him his traditional role.

O'Connor, the rising young Irish professional, was the current British match-play champion. More than equal to anybody in the other side, he seemed to be inspired greatly by this man-to-man stuff.

Eric Brown was the perfect man for the No. 1 spot, where Burke might be tempted to place one of his strong men. Brown, a hard Scot, still had a lot of grudges to work off. He had been made to wait several years before being allowed to play professional golf in Britain, and in that period of limbo he had proved his outstanding class frequently by winning the major Continental championships. When he was allowed into British golf, he played with a determined urgency which, although not exactly revenge, was prompted by the knowledge that he had a lot of catching up to do.

He had the professional's capacity to hate, momentarily of course, and to use that emotion to extend his skill and hone it to a lethal sharpness. In those days, too, he felt a little ill at ease in the stiff-necked world of golf, so far removed from his own early years as a railway worker.

He disliked the American professionals, by definition, because of their superiority and particularly because of the reverence they received from others, especially the Press. They were fair game for Brown, and Rees suspected that the Scot would dearly love to get his hands on Tommy Bolt, unquestionably the best player in the American side and almost certain to play in top position. If Rees could get that pairing at the top, and forestall a late counter-attack with his strong tail, then he felt there was room for hope.

The two captains were summoned to the ladies card-room in the Lindrick clubhouse to exchange their team lists, and Rees scanned the American order with increasing excitement. Bolt was in top place while Doug Ford, Dow Finsterwald and Dick Mayer had been lumped together in the tail. Rees had guessed it perfectly, and though the two captains talked for a few moments, Rees was anxious to return with the news.

As he walked into that dining-room he sensed that something was wrong. A group of men stood at the bar talking earnestly but in lowered voices and when they saw Rees, one turned on him and said: 'Harry Weetman has announced that he will not play again in a team captained by you!'

Suddenly Rees forgot his good news in this confusion. Weetman? Was it a joke? Weetman? He'd said he wasn't playing well. He'd agreed. Or they thought he'd agreed. Why hadn't he spoken in there? Why now, out here?

Rees wanted to find Weetman, but already events were overtaking him; there was a T.V. interview to be given, and by the time that was finished the team was back at the hotel. When Rees arrived there the Press were waiting for a statement.

Still, all that he knew had come to him second-hand, and

he could not check with Weetman. Now the Press were waiting for him to speak, and if there had been a chance that this episode could have been settled over a quiet drink, it was gone. The arena for this conflict would be the front page of almost every newspaper in the country.

What had changed Weetman's mind? If he disliked Rees, it really had nothing to do with this moment. Certainly the two men had little in common. Weetman was an amiable giant of a man who shunned the kind of popularity that Rees craved. He was a man of simple tastes, not given to flamboyance and distrustful of it in others.

It was a screen to hide something, and undoubtedly his actions suggested that he had no love for Rees. Ten years later, when Rees was nominated to lead a British team to the United States (Weetman had led the team in the home match but had not been given the away fixture as captain) Weetman again denounced Rees's leadership in a newspaper article.

The mystery of it all was that even this was not enough to prompt such an experienced professional knowingly to disturb the fragile morale of the British side by such a blatant attack on their leader. Whatever the merits of his case, that kind of attack at that precise moment could do only damage to the team, since it certainly would not relieve Rees of the captaincy in time to make any difference, even if anybody had listened to Weetman's points.

Weetman had left the team meeting apparently satisfied, and told some waiting friends that he had been dropped from the singles. That much is known, but the next stages of this regrettable episode, which led to the announcement, remained a secret that stayed with Weetman and went with him to his grave after a motor accident.

It was past midnight in their hotel when Rees gave orders that no more phone calls were to be put through to his room. The incident had flared into a major controversy, and Rees was uncertain how to react. For all that, he slept soundly,

169

and was down in the dining-room early the next morning to meet his men.

The papers were full of the 'Weetman Affair' which, combined with the reports of the pathetic first-day effort of the British, confirmed the dismal prospects of this day. And yet a curious transformation took place among these men as they sat around the breakfast tables reading their premature obituaries.

They had taken enough, and were sick of their role as no-hopers. They had been written-off from the start of this match and their patience now seemed exhausted. Weetman had not caused it, nor the confident Americans, nor the scathing Press. Rees's men suddenly tired of this script.

Rees now noticed that all of them were keyed up, tense, anxious to get into the fight, and their mood gave him even greater cause for hope, because the Americans would not expect this approach from what seemed a beaten side.

So it began, that final day, but not before Burke had made a last-minute and unprecedented request to put a replacement in his team for Ted Kroll, who felt ill. Rees was disappointed because Kroll had been something of a gift for the British side. He was not numbered among the best in the American group, and young Peter Mills, his opponent, had been fairly confident that he could handle him.

Rees could have claimed a walk-over, but that was unthinkable – or rather, it was thinkable but would cause too much criticism. So he agreed, and Burke accepted more than was offered by putting himself in Kroll's place. Burke had never been beaten in his long Ryder Cup service and the surprise had been, when the singles were announced, that he had decided against playing. If there had been second thoughts, then Kroll's illness was fortuitous and gave Burke a second chance to get it right.

The day had been ushered in by a cold easterly wind and Lindrick, though not a long course, had completely changed its character in this wind. The pace of the greens altered and offered more resistance, which might bemuse the Americans. Nobody really knew how they would react if they were hard pressed, since the foursomes had been virtually unconditional surrender by the British.

The hard core of the British side did not possess such force of shot, yet they had the virtue of straightness on a course that was hemmed in by punishing rough, particularly close to the greens. Bradshaw, O'Connor and Bousfield were craftsmen with a wedge, and strangely the Americans had shown signs of weakness with this particular stroke in practice and on the first day – although it had not mattered much.

This steadiness, combined with a sure touch and a hardening resolve, was to provide the perfect formula for success that day as the Americans tried desperately to fight two losing battles – one against the course, the other against their British opponents.

Brown and Bolt remain stiffly formal on the first tee. Both had intense pride, and while the match might have some importance to the team, the personal contest mattered more to both of them. Yet Bolt, no matter how desperately he wanted to beat Brown, found himself baffled by the wind, which undermined all his judgement of clubs, and bemused by the greens, whose stubbornness demanded a force of putt that the American was afraid to make. Bolt began to lose very early, and the word spread around the course.

Then, suddenly, the news was good everywhere, and the Americans were wilting under the strain. The supermen were in trouble – unable to escape and being ruthlessly hunted by these British golfers who had seemed so meek and amenable to defeat.

It was difficult not to become savagely nationalistic and see Brown as a fearless Scot leading the massacre, with the men around him drawing courage from his deeds and following him into the fight. The enemy were being cut to pieces. There was a short break for lunch. When it resumed, the

British team led in five matches, was square in one and trailed in the remaining two.

By now they were too involved in the fight, too excited by their own skill and the closeness of the triumph, to worry about how the roles had changed – how the meek British had suddenly erupted to crush their masters. Somehow those eight men had cast off the professional servility of a lifetime, and their individual frailty had been replaced by a strength of will that some would never experience in that measure again.

By mid-afternoon the cheering began, and the Americans were to complain afterwards that it was too partisan and loud when they missed a putt. The crowds, they claimed, were too pro-British – as if that should have surprised them!

But the cheering crowds gave more important evidence that there was no American counter-attack on the fairways of Lindrick. This was already a beaten team that could not find the necessary respite from the conflict to restore its confidence. The situation for them was impossible to handle since, theoretically, it could not happen.

The British crowd surged jubilantly over the course, and it was estimated that at least 6,000 people entered without paying, because the men on the gates ran out of tickets. But nobody, except P.G.A. officials, cared; all were caught up in this glorious moment.

Almost everywhere offered a story of triumph. Even young Mills, so apprehensive at facing the great Jackie Burke, watched in amazement as the American handed him victory through a series of errors. Brown had reduced Bolt to a state of near apoplexy, and by the end of the day the American's wedge lay in pieces, a poor substitute for Eric Brown. In the gathering gloom, the American casualty rate increased, Rees and Bousfield put their men down, and young Bernard Hunt crushed Doug Ford, a gnarled campaigner, with a five-hole lead.

O'Connor heaped the agonies upon Finsterwald, and was

seven up. The width of the margins added to the fantasy, and the Americans had clearly surrendered but were unable to find a white flag. Hunt, by poetic justice, tapped in the putt that gave Britain victory and thereby erased all shadow of blame for his Wentworth error. By the end of the day only one point had been lost.

Rees was ecstatic, because in twenty-four hours he had experienced almost every human feeling from depression, through confusion, sadness, anger, hope and joy, to an unabashed pride in himself and his men. Nevertheless, some of the sadness remained as he thought about Weetman. The man had taken his rightful place at the presentation of the trophy yet the consequences of his outburst had not been forgotten.

Rees was asked for an official report, which he submitted to the Professional Golfers Association. It led to Weetman's suspension from tournament golf, arguments about the legality of restricting his trade, and subsequently his reinstatement.

Sadly, Lindrick changed nothing, except that the Americans never treated the Ryder Cup as lightly again and ensured that their best players represented their country in future matches. At best, it gave the British cause for hope. It proved that on a cold grey autumn afternoon in Yorkshire, a bunch of men found within themselves the kind of faith that moves mountains. If nothing else, it was a start.

Chapter 18: *Tony Lema,*
St Andrews, 1964

The yacht was anchored that night in Mobile Bay; it was late, and Arnold Palmer wanted to sleep. But Lema, in the other bunk, wanted to talk, or rather, he wanted Palmer to talk. Tomorrow, when they reached West Palm Beach for another tournament, it would be too late. Palmer would step back into his legend, oblige every outstretched hand, smile at every camera and march at the head of his army. But here and now he was the man in the next bunk, so removed from that image that Lema had to remind himself that the lifeless form across the other side of the cabin was the greatest figure in present-day golf, and probably in its history.

It was 1960, and they were guests on board after the Mobile Open, which Palmer had won that day. He had also captured the U.S. Masters, the U.S. Open and missed the British Open by only one stroke – and most of those titles had resulted from his brazen last-minute rush when somebody else's hand was on the trophy.

Lema was a supporting act, still struggling to master his swing and temperament into an obedience that would bring the success that others predicted for him. But he was impatient. What was Palmer's secret? How could he suddenly lift his game to an inspired pitch and sweep everybody out of his way?

What was the difference between the two of them? Even Palmer had to admit that Lema's swing was better. And yet why wasn't that enough? How could Palmer produce that blinding brilliance to win?

Palmer gazed drowsily at the ceiling. It was a confusing line of interrogation because Lema was really asking him why he was Arnold Palmer. He had never really thought about it. To him, it was like breathing, it happened and he never questioned it.

'I kind of see what I have to do,' he mused, 'and I just make up my mind I'm going to do it If I have to make a long putt then I shut out all thoughts of missing it . . .'

Lema waited for more, then realised that the man was asleep. He considered Palmer's words, and was not sure whether they had been profound or nothing more than the last scrambled thoughts of a man slipping into unconsciousness. Perhaps Palmer's words simply underlined a truth he already knew but could not prove himself; that winning was a state of mind which embraced the fact before it happened. It was a view of the future which possessed all the certainty of the present, as though the time factor had disappeared.

Or was it the ability to make things happen? To see the target, then to pursue it with single-minded ruthlessness? If Lema could not yet do this on a golf course, his own life was actual proof that he could change what appeared to be a rigid destiny.

His father had been a Portugese immigrant labourer in Oakland and had died when Anthony David Lema was three years old. The family lived in a tough district, and it seemed that only two destinies awaited him. If the surrounding petty pilfering, street fights and other delinquent tendencies did not push him into a life of crime, then there was always the local cannery, where he could pass a repetitious existence until old age.

His delinquency, or rather his desire for easy money, first took him to a golf course, where he joined the other kids in the caddie shed of the local municipal course. It revealed the good life beyond his own tough neighbourhood, and the natural athlete picked up the golf technique with

accomplished ease – and realised that this was to be his pass-
port out of the slums of Oakland.

That was the target, and he pursued it first with a job as
an assistant professional in San Francisco, then as a full
teaching professional – and in between he served two years
with the Marines in Korea. He knew then that he had
escaped from his twin destinies in Oakland. He had believed
this to be so long before it happened – just as Palmer regarded success on a golf course.

Lema dwelt upon this coincidence there in the bunk, and
the memories of all his failures, the first-hand knowledge
of his constant weakness, made him realise that it would be
a long haul to reach Palmer's state of mind.

Lema had much more to conquer. His own Latin temperament glittered with inspirational brilliance, but more
often brought on a suicidal impetuosity. When he had joined
the American professional tour, sponsored by a businessman
who saw some potential in him, he had finished that first
futile season with debts of 11,000 dollars. It bothered the
businessman more than it did Lema, who had little regard
for money as long as there was some in his pocket.

It had taken time, but the shell of composure began to
harden around him, although there were the occasional
cracks, such as the episode in the hotel room when they all
got roaring drunk and fired full-blooded drives out the window and down the main street. He realised that he could not
hurry the process of success, and that perhaps he would not
know when he was ready until it happened. Suddenly, somewhere, it would all fall into place.

The night in that yacht in Mobile Bay had been long
forgotten before Lema's destiny began to take shape. He had
been around for five years, a permanent background feature,
when suddenly his golf came together and he produced con-
secutive and consistent winning play.

It earned him a lot of money, and in 1963 he collected
24,000 dollars in prize money and dutifully handed over to

the businessman his share of the winnings. But as Lema began to earn more, the prospect of handing over even more cash seemed to frustrate him. He had been happy enough to accept the sponsorship that allowed him to play but now it seemed to drain his resources and his spirit.

The sponsor paid him a weekly wage and kept half the winnings, and now Lema resolved to buy himself out of the contract. The price was £17,000. But in 1964 he was still producing superb golf and earned enough to buy his freedom, so that when he arrived at St. Andrews for the British Open he was, in his own words, a free man.

He had arrived late and given himself no time for proper preparation. St Andrews is notorious as the graveyard of great golfers, and even Bobby Jones had detested it until, through the passage of time and much failure, he had learned how to play the course.

Peter Thomson the Australian respected the Old Course as the absolute test in golf skill, which combined demands of correct judgement and flawless skill. The Old Course itself was quite unlike anything Lema had seen in his life, an apparently desolate tract, void of plant life, packed with craters and swept by cold gnawing winds and frequent rain.

The general opinion in every pub in town was that Lema had left it too late, because this course could not be learned in such a short time, and there was no doubt that it had to be learned – it was littered with perils, and all of them had to be charted.

Lema had to shake off the shattering effect of the trans-Atlantic time change, capture the technique of hitting the smaller golf ball, and revise the striking distance of every club in his bag in a variety of weather conditions. It was too much to accomplish in the one remaining day before the championship began, but Lema made good newspaper copy if only because of the reputation he brought to St Andrews.

Within an hour of his arrival he was out on the course, and Palmer, who was not playing that year, arranged for his local caddie to work for Lema. It was an important alliance, for this humourless, solemn-faced Scot, Tip Anderson, was to play a major role in that championship.

Lema had done himself a curious kind of favour by arriving late. This was indeed a treacherous golf course, yet in the time available to him he could not appreciate all its terrors. In any case it is doubtful whether a more protracted preparation would have served any purpose but to frighten him, and by the time he had begun to assemble some idea of the perils of the Old Course he was launched favourably into the championship.

He relied heavily on the advice and judgement of his caddie. (That was his way, and even a year later at Birkdale, when he beheld the short twelfth for the first time, he turned to his caddie, a new man, and said: 'I shall put my hand out and you put the right club in it.' Willie Aitchison replied: 'I'll put the right club there. Just you hit it right.' The ball was drilled within a few feet of the flag).

There was, of course, another factor in his favour, because not only was he in the middle of an inspired spell, but also he had a manageable perspective on the British Open. He was not overwhelmed by it, and was still not convinced that a decent tournament win at home would not be better for him.

Had he taken it more seriously, he would have arrived earlier. While this was the championship all the great men had won – Hogan, Snead, Sarazen, Jones – Lema was immune to the kind of stifling stage fright that drags many men below their best when they tee up to compete in the British Open.

His first look at St Andrews told him that the wedge would be the most useless club in his bag that week. The greens were as receptive as concrete and down-wind they offered no sanctuary for an airborne stroke. That week, he knew, he would need to pitch and run the ball, accepting the perils of the bumps and bad bounces in order to keep the ball moving towards – and somewhere on – the greens.

The championship began with Lema regarding Anderson with the implicit trust a blind man shows to his guide dog. Whatever Anderson advised, Lema concurred and had the talent to observe with fractional precision. Just how superior that talent was, he demonstrated on the first day through a 50 m.p.h. gale which tore into the hearts and determination of most of other men. Lema emerged two strokes behind the leaders.

The wind lessened on the second day, and Lema found his stride with a 68 which seemed to ruin the legend of the Old Course, since he could still be regarded as conducting his practice rounds, which just happened to be part of the championship. Certainly he could not know St Andrews the way he should, yet that did not seem to affect his score.

On the last day, Lema was clear, and launched himself into a cautious protection of his lead. It was a ruinous tactic because his very defensiveness seemed to squander strokes. He stumbled badly, then received a frightening jolt.

He looked at the scoreboard, and realised that Nicklaus, who had started the day nine strokes behind him, was now one shot away. Lema fought the depressing feeling that he had thrown it all away. He could see what he had to do. But could he do it? Of course, Palmer, those years ago in Mobile, had said it was possible, that will power produced the reality. But this was not Palmer. This was Lema.

He had played the opening six holes of that third round in pathetic fashion, yet the news of Nicklaus spurred him into action and transformed his golf, so that his figures for the remaining holes were 333–334–443–443. It was a 68 which put seven strokes between himself and Nicklaus, who now shrugged his shoulders in resignation. Lema had indeed seen what had to be done – and he had done it.

He could not be caught now, and even the Old Course seemed to surrender, as the wind dropped to take all the terror from the closing holes. In that last round, there was no challenge to be answered, and Lema guided his ball with tedious skill back to the clubhouse, convinced that others would not take the risks to catch him.

Just once, he treated the crowd to a moment of drama, when he stood ankle-deep in rough on the side of a hill after hooking his ball from the tee. Yet he selected his four-wood and clipped the ball free so that it drilled, then curved into the green close enough for a birdie.

Long before he arrived at the last hole, the champagne had been delivered to the Press tent to perpetuate the custom that Lema initiated at his first tournament win in the United States. It had earned him the nickname Champagne Tony, a fitting label for a man who escaped the slums of Oakland and would have fitted perfectly behind a Wall Street desk or in some American embassy.

If there were any doubts as to how and why Lema had won this British Open, then he resolved them all with his final stroke of the championships. His drive left him 50 yards from the green, and he reached for his seven-iron to nudge the ball through the Valley of Sin in front of the green and leave it two feet from the hole.

It had been the perfect stroke for St Andrews, and it demonstrated that he possessed not only the instinct but also the comprehensive skill to adjust to whatever special demands a golf course presented. That made him a rare man, and his courtly manner added to a personal magnetism gave him a public appeal which perhaps only Palmer of that generation of American golfers exceeded. That is the lingering memory, in the years after he and his wife were killed in an aeroplane crash.

Chapter 19: *Gary Player, Carnoustie, 1968*

The Press were waiting for him, and Player had no idea how they knew that he would arrive at Carnoustie a week early. But they spotted him before he reached the newly-built clubhouse, and Player was irritated, because he had wanted it to be different and to work quietly and privately once the local people had become accustomed to him. Now the Press had seen him there would be no solitude.

The questions were the same. How did he explain his bad year? Was that the reason for arriving a week before the Open began? Was it his kind of course? Was he any happier with his game?

It was the customary charade in which they, as much as he, knew there were no real answers, and that he *had* finished high in a dozen tournaments, and there *was* no real reason why he had not won, except that the pieces did not fall into place. It was not worthy of speculation, since it was one of those things that happens in a professional's life.

'I have never played better golf in my life for so long without winning a tournament. I am here a week early, but even that isn't long enough to prepare properly for a British Open. Look how long Hogan took to get ready. That's the way it should be done. But I have a schedule to keep which doesn't permit me much time in any one place – especially at home with my family . . .'

Their heads were bowed as they scribbled earnestly in their notebooks, satisfied with this stuff, and tomorrow's sports pages would give Player the 'arrival treatment'. All got it –

Palmer, Nicklaus, Casper – and it seemed at times that they timed their arrivals to avoid a clash, so that each could monopolise the headlines for at least one morning during those days before a championship, when the Pressmen, in their fashion, were as edgy as the players.

The talk droned on, and Player knew the answers by heart, yet seemed able to listen to his own voice as if hearing them for the first time. Alfie Fyles, his caddie, waited patiently at the back of the crowd, the shoes and clubs ready for work.

Player looked beyond the Pressman, and instructed Alfie to wait outside, where he would join him in a minute. It was the signal for the interview to end. The Press accepted the decision meekly and trooped out. One of them stayed behind, but then one of them always does, in the hope of an additional snippet which the others have missed.

At least they had kept off apartheid, but then that question was not really the concern of these sports journalists. It was always difficult to explain his reason for his declared support for South Africa's policy of racial segregation. What he felt seemed perfectly justifiable, and yet the feelings lost something in their transmission. In any case, it seemed unfair that, because of his skill as a golfer, he should be called upon wherever he travelled to justify this policy. Did Palmer or Nicklaus ever have to justify Vietnam? Or the coloured problem? Nobody ever thought to ask them.

He left the clubhouse to play golf, and his first taste of Carnoustie made him happy that he had arrived a week early. He suspected that this was the toughest course he had ever seen. It was a long unforgiving links which had become more spiteful because the rough had been allowed to advance to the edges of the fairway.

The local people were proud of its forbidding reputation – Carnoustie to them was the true home of modern golf. From this tiny fishing village, three hundred young golfers had emigrated at the turn of the century to teach and play the game all over the world. There was, so they said, a Carnoustie swing, on which the modern technique was based, and the great Bobby Jones himself had learned the Carnoustie style from his mentor Stuart Maiden, a local lad who had emigrated to the United States. If Carnoustie was responsible for some of the best golfers in the world, then it seemed correct that the Scottish village should possess one of the strictest tests of golf on God's Earth.

Player's early practice at Carnoustie brought home another painful fact to him. He realised that his Ping-style putter was dreadfully out of tune and felt so awkward in his hands that he was more aware of its clumsiness than the engrossing task of holing a putt.

It was time to change, but the only other putter in which he had any trust was back home in Johannesburg. That evening he made his usual telephone call to his wife, who was due to arrive just before the championship, and asked her to bring over the blade putter which he had acquired in Japan six years earlier.

But even when his wife arrived with the putter, there seemed to be no improvement. Something had gone wrong, but he could not trace the fault. He could see the line of each putt perfectly, and although he felt he had made the correct stroke, the ball chose a route of its own.

He grumbled openly about his putting; it was so terrible, and yet there is something about bad putting that never makes it one's own fault. It is like a headache or a boil in that it belongs to you and you can grumble about it, but it is not your fault. But then nothing is ever the professional's fault. It cannot be. No professional will ever admit, even to himself, that he was inferior, or that somebody really played better or is better. The other man had the run of the ball and the good fortune and that was the essential difference. It is, in most cases, a deep conviction and form of self-defence for the best golfers.

Player knew that, without his putting on this course, he

was lost, because Nicklaus and Palmer had the power to cope with these long fairways, and he would be stretched to a waywardness that could only be redeemed by a sure putting touch.

The paradox was to be that this uncertain mood offered him his best chance of success. Player already accepted that he would have to fight Carnoustie every inch of the way and therein, though he did not realise it, lay the only effective strategy for success on this course.

This time there were to be no premonitions, no real cause for hope nor mystical signs on the scoreboard as there were in his mind when he won the U.S. Open at Bellerive and 'saw' his name as winner long before the championship finished. This was going to be a week of hard work, and perhaps nothing better than an opportunity to honour his many commercial contracts in Britain.

The championship began, and for most of that week he was sustained by his own professionalism and experience, which kept him close to the leaders even though he had not played particularly well. But even in this state of affairs there was a glint of hope, because it meant that Carnoustie was not yielding without a fight. But he did not feel like a winner and his own golf had been generally a matter of tidy salvage work. He was too preoccupied with the job in hand to consider his prospects.

Yet, with surprise and gratification, he found himself close to the leaders at the start of the last day. It had seemed to be a duel between Casper and Charles, the New Zealander, but their lead was not large enough to hold any significance, and as such could be lost on one hole. Nobody would escape without some damage; therefore Player, just behind them, or even Nicklaus, was just as dangerous in the fight that would ensue.

This last round would be as confused as a bar-room brawl – all action, no pattern, with each man fighting as hard as he knew, and only when the dust had settled would they see who was left standing. Player had scrapped with Carnoustie all week, so today would be little different. He had worked the ball around the course, protecting his weaknesses, accepting the punishments and hitting back when he could.

In terms of that championship title, neither Charles nor Casper were the real dangers, since at that time in their careers there was a general, and unfair, suspicion that they were men too cautious to grab titles, but always ready to step out of the shadows should somebody else make a mistake in the act of winning.

Nicklaus had made a nonsense of the last two holes at Lytham in 1963 when Charles seemed a certain runner-up, yet the New Zealander found himself in a play-off for the title with an equally surprised Phil Rodgers the next day. Palmer had thrown away a five-stroke lead in four holes of the 1966 U.S. Open at Olympic, and Casper had gratefully picked up the pieces.

Both golfers were outstanding putters, and while that talent might have won other championships it was only part of the attack needed at Carnoustie, whose fairways had to be fought all the way for the privilege of putting on its greens. It demanded a more comprehensive repertoire of stroke-making, and that meant Jack Nicklaus, who had the power and the accuracy. Player's only comfort was that he had been paired with the American, and so would know at first-hand what the pace would be.

The first hint that Nicklaus was not in full command of his power came on the long sixth hole, which is flanked on the left by a rifle range. It needed a big drive from Nicklaus if he was to get home with any comfort with his next blow, and he deemed it worth the risk of unleashing the ball at terrifying speed into that narrowing fairway. In any case, by now Nicklaus was closing on the leaders, who were in trouble, and it was not the time to play safe.

He grunted with the effort he put into the drive, and the ball took off too much in the centre of the fairway, because

Nicklaus knew that this ball had been hit with draw and that once the power had left it, the spin would carry it down towards the left and the rifle range.

The ball soared high, a black speck in that grey sky, and the crowd waited for the first sign of a suicidal drift to the left. Then it began to move.

For a moment there was a hopeful confused silence, but then they waved from up the fairway and it was clear that Nicklaus's ball was out of bounds. He spun in anger and kicked hard at his golf bag. His astonished caddie Jimmy Dickinson let go of the bag, and it fell to the ground. Dickinson felt obliged to apologise, then realised that it was not his fault, and looked disgruntled. Immediately Nicklaus was embarrassed, because he never liked to show that it mattered that much to him.

Dickinson gave him another golf ball; he tried again, and this time it was perfect, drilled to the right, then eating up the fairway as it moved back into the middle. But it was too late, and by the time they trooped from that green, Player found himself leading the British Open for the first time that week. Casper had lost all sense of purpose, it seemed, and Charles was engaged too heavily in fighting the course.

Player was exhilarated, but tormented by doubt, because he was a long way from the clubhouse. There was much treachery still to be overcome, and his golf was not at its best. Nicklaus would certainly revive and mount a fierce attack over the longer finishing holes. And yet there was no point to his fear, since the manner in which he had struggled had brought him to the front, and there was no reason to think that it would not sustain him.

Anyway, he had nothing better to offer and no other way to play. He would contrive to keep himself going, because nobody was finding it easy and his own stamina might just be greater than theirs. That, at least, was his hope and his reason to keep trying.

But by the time Charles and Casper had completed the thirteenth hole, they had drawn level with Player, who had drilled his drive too far left, so that it was blocked on that fourteenth fairway by two sandhills called The Spectacles, from which the hole derives its name.

Nicklaus had steered his own drive away from the hills, but had aimed too wide of them, and was trapped among trees on the right. The American could see very little, and certainly had no view of the green. He selected a three-wood, and from the depths lashed hard at the ball – then waited and listened. The noise from the crowd would tell him whether it had been good or bad.

Then the cheering began, low at first, then gathering to a crescendo as his ball scrambled on the green. It had been a magnificent stroke which had earned him at least the chance of a birdie.

Player looked down at his own ball. If he jumped in the air he could just see the tip of the long flagstick, but once settled over the ball the shot had to be played from memory, and he had to be certain that the ball cleared those hills in the first few split-seconds of its life.

He knew now that Nicklaus had begun to press as hard as Charles and Casper, who were now waiting on the fourteenth tee to play. This was the moment when he could submerge under the pressure; when their golf and his lack of form could conspire to make his time as leader of that championship nothing more than a tantalising accident.

It was enough to inspire him as he attempted to distil the knowledge and skill of a lifetime into that next stroke. He opened up, jack-knifed into his backswing, then grimaced as the club met the ball with furious power. Then he, too, could only wait and listen as the ball disappeared over the hills.

Then it came again. But this time the roar was louder – then it was a shriek, and he galloped to the top of the hill to see what had happened. He was still not sure, but everybody was waving, so he knew that the ball must be close to the flag.

He marched towards the cheers, then saw the reason. His ball was no more than two feet from the hole. If ever one stroke won a championship, then this was it! It gave Player an eagle three, an operating margin over Nicklaus and the other two, but more important it broke their spirits in that extreme moment of tension.

Nothing could stop Player now, not even an enormous drive of 300 yards from Nicklaus down the last hole while the South African carefully picked his way with his irons to his second British Open. Hogan had been right. It was best to come early to Carnoustie.

Chapter 20: *Henry Cotton, Royal St George's 1934*

There was a neat irony to this moment. Cotton had been forced to sit alone in this tent while the thousands who had come to see him win settled down. Yet the delay they were causing was ruining him, and might be the very reason he did not win.

He was so far ahead, with the last round of the British Open to be played, that nothing could go wrong. But now, as he sat alone beside the first tee at Royal St. George's, hidden from prying eyes in this tent, he was confronted by the only problem for which he had no solution. He had been given time to think, time to dwell upon a hundred possibilities, none specific, but all disastrous, and all with the same nightmare of Cotton losing the championship which he should have won by a mile.

The man who is destined to win lives in those moments in a world between fantasy and reality, and this spell is fragile. Once broken it cannot be repaired, because so many forces and nuances and hours have been used to contrive it; its manufacture is lengthy.

The spell had now been shattered for Cotton. It should have been a dream that somehow he was able to control, an enduring yet manageable hysteria which permitted him greater capacity of action. So it would have been, if his thousands of devoted followers had not sentenced him to fifteen minutes alone with himself in a tent.

The greatest moment of his life was within reach, and yet now, he suspected that it was not. At lunchtime he was so far ahead that they had congratulated him and he had tried to shut his ears to them, lest the gods overheard and damned him for his presumption. So long as he had been borne along by the tide of events, yet playing his part, it had remained a reasonable contest. But he could not fight the nightmares, each feasible and from his own knowledge of his temperament quite within reason.

For ten years he had been trying to win this British Open, and while nobody would argue that he was not the best golfer in Britain, and of late had even touched world-class, he could never deliver the documented proof of that fact with his name on the trophy.

This failure was sufficient ammunition for his critics, who could argue that, while he manifested all the arrogance of a champion, he had no right to that posture so long as he could not deliver the goods.

His critics had been plentiful from the start of his career, when, as a public schoolboy, he chose professional golf as a career and thus broke the monopoly of talented artisans. He was a renegade from the middle class, and not accepted fully by his chosen fraternity. Not that this bothered him; indeed he preferred it. But he was, therefore, a man who defied social definition, since he had the pedigree and affluence of a gent but was toiling in the domain of the working class.

It might have been mistaken for a pioneering spirit, but Cotton never saw it as such. He believed that the skilled professional – be he lawyer, surgeon, engineer or golfer – was not only worthy of his hire, but also of even greater rewards if he could do it better than most other people.

Nobody in British golf ever worked harder to master the golf swing, and Cotton forced himself to endless practice that was to leave his body warped for life by the hours he toiled. This gnawing desire for self-improvement and the success it would bring drove him at a frantic pace, and whatever pain he endured was ignored. So, too, were his meals as he remained working and working on the practice ground.

He had been spurred on in this task by his first sight of American golf and how the top sportsmen were regarded as having equal status with any other profession. He had seen the great Walter Hagen treated as regally as a film star – and acting as such – and saw no reason for this attitude not to exist in Britain.

But the differences between himself and Hagen were enormous. Firstly, Hagen was a champion, and secondly the higher social strata of American life was made up largely of self-made men – the Fords and Chryslers – blacksmiths who had built cars in their workshops and founded empires. They accepted a man as they found him, and respected his success, whatever his chosen field.

Cotton faced a more rigid social order in Britain, and while he could live magnificently outside it, he knew that he could not be taken seriously until he was a champion. This showed itself in so many ways; he was, for example, clearly one of the best golfers in the world, yet he could charge no more for a golf lesson than a caddie would to carry clubs for a round.

This was his frustration, and all his other success could not change the situation. He knew that one British Open would set new standards for him overnight. Only then could he really break this condescending attitude towards the professional golfer and earn his true rewards.

He wanted cash, he wanted respect, and he was scrupulously aware of his own status within the profession. He refused to play for the 1931 Ryder Cup side because they refused him permission to stay on and play in the U.S. Open. He declined to play in an English international side because it interfered with his British Open preparations – but even then he had failed, as Sarazen won the title and he languished far behind.

In the same year, he took the decision that was to change the course of his life. He resolved to quit Btitain and take a professional's job in Belgium. He needed to break the ties and, anyway, he received more respect on the Continent. The Open itself was becoming a lost cause, and with each failure it seemed to grow in its impossibility and importance.

The decision heaped fresh criticism upon him, which itself convinced him that he needed time away from this constant critical attention, where even the simplest act on his part was studied for some devious implication. At the same time, he wondered whether he was making the right decision.

Then he received a letter which convinced him of its correctness. Sandy Herd, one of the great father-figures of British golf, and one of the few men Cotton respected, wrote urging Cotton to forget the critics and go where the money was, because 'far too many people wanted too much for too little'.

His time in Belgium held immense therapeutic value, for not only did it restore his flagging health, but also he returned to the 1934 British Open at Royal St George's, Sandwich, with a new perspective on the championship. It had been in his thoughts all year, and yet being removed from the immediate atmosphere gave him time to build his confidence and – more important – his keenness to play.

But that confidence vanished when he arrived at the course and realised that he was playing awful golf. He had brought with him four sets of clubs, but this luxury of choice served only to confuse him, and the more he experimented the worse his golf became. He felt so dispirited that it occurred to him to withdraw, and beat a hasty retreat to Belgium. Thoroughly despondent, he cut short his practice on Saturday afternoon, threw his clubs into the car, and vowed not to hit another stroke until the qualifying rounds on the Monday.

Only when he came to play in the pre-qualifying did he realise how important that respite for his worries had been, for he produced such artistry in a 66 that it seemed a shame to waste such brilliance on such an ordinary chore as getting into the championship.

The good golf had been just under the surface all the time, and a break from the frustrating sequence of practice in which nothing seemed to go right was the only possible antidote. To have carried on with his practice would have driven him only more deeply into a depression that was really unnecessary.

It is the way of all truly great competitors to undergo a transformation once the bell goes, once the playing itself is for real. It is a change over which the competitor has no control; his skill begins to function with a new purpose which is impossible to stimulate artificially. The reality of the championship is the essential impetus.

For Cotton there was to be a reaction to his brilliant first round, and he ambled around the neighbouring Deal course in 75 strokes, partly because he did not play well, but mostly because there was no incentive. That first round had seen him comfortably into the championship, and now the scores would be scrapped.

Nor did that 75 represent his true form, because he knew that he was playing as well as he had ever done, and that every department of his game was under strict control and working at peak efficiency. Just as certainly as he had known at St Andrews last season that even though he led going into the last round it would 'not be his year', he knew now that everything was perfect.

On the first day, he dismissed St George's in 67 strokes, then, like a man correcting his earlier mistakes, went out the next day and produced a 65, so that he wondered why he had ever thought this game so difficult and how the British Open had ever seemed that difficult to win.

He was now seven strokes clear, and already in no doubt that he could – and would – win. The last day, bathed in sunshine and cooled by a gentle breeze, opened for him with a 72 to put him nine strokes clear. That round had been no different in playing standards between tee and green than his earlier efforts, but now he could not summon the urgency nor transmit it to his putter on the greens. It simply was not needed.

And then they had left him alone in the tent before the start of the final round, and he had time to dwell upon the effort, the controversies, the criticism, the failures, and the other things that had brought him to this moment.

He knew that, because of his temperament, he was a man of extremes who could not work within narrow margins of efficiency. With Cotton it was either brilliant or awful, and for most of that week it had been brilliant.

Now he had time to contemplate the possibility of the awful part, and he panicked as he realised that maybe the thought itself was enough to bring it on. He broke out in a cold sweat as he could not shake this thought from his mind. His stomach twisted into a tight knot, so cramped that he had difficulty standing up when they called him to play.

He tried to convince himself that the triumph was less than three hours away. But the thought was not strong enough, and all that remained was an awareness of how this could go wrong, and what awful golf he had brought to Sandwich that week.

He thought of all the people flanking the fairways waiting for him to win, assuming they were watching a formality, witnesses to a lap of honour. How dare they be so certain? His other scores – the 67 and the 65 and even the 72 – now seemed the work of another man. Not Cotton, this wretched creature racked with pain and cramp, who wondered now whether he could find the strength to walk around the course.

As he emerged from the tent, he heard the surprised murmurings in the crowd as they beheld this ashen man on the point of collapse. It crossed his mind to tell them he could not go on with it, and he had visions of himself falling unconscious over a stroke on some fairway. But what then? How long would they give him to recover?

So he teed up the ball and began to play. What he had

experienced was the cold fear that lurks within every man's breast when he is put to such an extreme test. It remains locked there in the heat of the conflict because there are so many other things to think about in the process of deliverance. Such fear would have remained mercifully concealed from Cotton, had he not been given a quarter of an hour alone.

The fear had savaged his composure, and his golf was painfully erratic and grossly ineffective. He nibbled at the course where before he had devoured it in great chunks. He scattered strokes with frightening disregard, and had used 40 to cope with the front nine holes.

He was frightened because he knew that he was slipping back into the field. Yet he was powerless to stop this suicide to which he was an unwilling but ever-present witness. He turned for home, and there seemed to be no change of fortune. He was slipping fast, and there was nothing to save him. On the thirteenth green he looked set to take another five when he left the ball ten feet from the hole. His putting had been awful, and not once had he made an aggressive move against the course. He was now looking for redemption – and having very little luck finding it.

He jabbed wearily at the ten-footer, because no amount of preparation or study seemed to improve the accuracy of his putting. He waited forlornly for this one to miss as the others had done. But it didn't. It hit the back of the hole and, as if jumping with delight that Cotton had at last remembered what to do, spun into the air then dropped back into the hole.

It was to be his salvation, a sign that he could still slow down if not reverse his failing fortunes. He played steadily back to the clubhouse for a 79 and a total of 283 to become champion. That he could afford the luxury of such a high score in the final round reflects the brilliant standard of his early play and how he had shattered the opposition, because he was still to win by five strokes.

Now, with triumph, it would all change. He had made his mark, and as he listened to the speeches and the praise at the prize giving, he was grateful for it, yet impatient for it all to stop. He had a more important task on his mind.

When it was over he took the trophy and slipped away to the nearby Guilford Hotel. In one of the rooms an old man was waiting, as Cotton knew he would be. All week this ailing man had forced himself painfully to the course and had sat beside The Maiden, the short hole, waiting for Cotton to pass. But the old man had been too sick to leave his bed for this, the last day.

Cotton knocked on the door and walked in. Harry Vardon was still in his bed. Cotton gave him the trophy without speaking, and Vardon looked at it and began to weep. Perhaps it was the joy at meeting an old friend, for this trophy had been his for six years and nobody had bettered that record.

Perhaps too the trophy was a reminder of glories past, of the great names that had been part of his life, of his own talent on which modern golf was based, and of the infirmities which now trapped him. Cotton wept too. For him it was a beginning. And Vardon knew that too.

INDEX